Human Values in Education

RUDOLF STEINER

HUMAN VALUES IN EDUCATION

Ten Lectures
Given in Arnheim (Holland) July 17-24 1924

Translated by Vera Compton-Burnett

1971
RUDOLF STEINER PRESS
35 Park Road, London NW1

First published 1971

The German text of the following lectures is published under the title *Der pädagogische Wert der Menschenerkenntnis und der Kulturvert der Pädagogik* in volume No. 310 of the Complete Centenary Edition of the Works of Rudolf Steiner (from the section comprising lectures and courses on Education).

This English edition is published by permission of the *Rudolf Steiner Nachlassverwaltung*, Dornach, Switzerland.

All Rights Reserved

© Rudolf Steiner Press, London, 1971

ISBN 0 85440 250 0

MADE AND PRINTED IN GREAT BRITAIN BY
THE GARDEN CITY PRESS LIMITED
LETCHWORTH, HERTFORDSHIRE
SG6 1JS

FOREWORD

The year 1924 in which these lectures were given was the last of Rudolf Steiner's active life as a lecturer and was indeed cut short by illness at the end of September. But during those nine months he gave an almost unbelievable variety of lectures, including courses on Life after Death, on Karmic relations, on Truth and Error in Spiritual Investigation, on Christian Festivals, on Eurythmy in its two aspects as interpreter of both Speech and Music, on Speech and Drama, on Medicine (for Doctors) on Theology (for Priests) and on Agriculture (for Farmers). Many of these were given in Dornach in the so-called "Carpenter's Shop" where work had been done for the first Goetheanum and close to which the new Goetheanum was rising from the ashes of the old. Others, however, were given in places as far apart as Stuttgart, Berne, Prague, Koberwitz, Paris, Arnheim, Torquay and London.

In addition to the great variety of subjects listed above were five courses on Education, given in five different places, of which that here printed was the penultimate, the last being the course for English teachers in Torquay, published under the title *The Kingdom of Childhood*.

When Steiner was in Torquay for this last course, he remarked to the teachers for whom he gave it that the English do not like long names and titles. The full German title of the lectures in this volume is *The Educational Value of the Knowledge of Man and the Cultural Value of Education*. Prompted, as it may be said, by Rudolf Steiner himself the Translator and Publishers have ventured to give them the shorter title of *Human Values in Education*. For this is their constantly recurring theme. We make educational programmes and systems but in making them we constantly forget the human spiritual and cultural values by which the child, the teacher and civilisation itself can only truly live. In Steiner's view it is man who gives significance to the world : and the lectures contain the terrible indictment that "the world significance of modern education is that it is gradually undermining the significance of the world". The lectures show the way to restoring to man the significance of the world and to the world the significance of man.

A.C.H.

GUIDE TO CONTENTS

Lecture I ...   .   Page 13

Anthroposophical Education based on a knowledge of man. Theoretical knowledge fails in life, as illustrated in business affairs and medicine. External educational psychology does not understand the living child. Love the first essential in education. Child descends from spiritual worlds by divine grace. Cleverness of modern education programmes. No programme in Waldorf School, only teachers and children. Relation between the physical and the soul-spiritual in childhood differs from that in adult. Old age in early epochs. Maturation regresses in history. Greek relation to sculpture. Genius in childhood. Teacher compared to a gardener.

Lecture II   ...   .   Page 28

Experiences in childhood may not produce their effects till the fifties. Need to understand effect of experience in spiritual world exemplified by Goethe and Schiller. Goethe's difficulty in entering body, but his subsequent good health and good looks. Long trunk and short legs a sign of harmonious adaptation to the body. Productive power in the middle of Goethe's life. Schiller's disharmony with his body. His ugly head, long legs, and weak rhythmic system, leading to cramps. All this due to stoppages in the fulfilment of karma. Similar conditions illustrated in acquaintance of Steiner, who also could not bring experience of spiritual world into physical. He suffered from stutter and squint and died after operation for the latter at 30. He would have had difficulty in developing consciousness soul at 35. Schiller prevented from finishing things by his cramp. The "Malteser" and "Demetrius". Mystery of his death. Importance of listening to children's voices.

Lecture III   ...   .   Page 48

Importance of stages of childhood. Fine distinctions necessary. Mother's milk mediates child into world into which he grows in first seven years. Movement, gesture and imitation characterise this period. Distinction in early movements. Speech arises from movement. Vowels. Consonants. Religious devotion to world reaches to the physical body. Environment affects child's organism. The counting horse explained. After seven comes feeling for coordination and for speech, which arises from gesture. Authority of teacher vital. Teaching immortality through the symbol of the butterfly. Letters to be introduced as pictures. Two theories of origin of a speech. Outer and inner harmonised in consonants and vowels. Examples of picture letters. Realistic dolls condemned. "Study of Man" at ten or eleven and its effect on modelling. Greek artists and the model. Living teaching necessary. A question answered.

Lecture IV ... ... Page 71

A question concerning imitation from a very young age. Reflection of the three epochs of childhood in gesture, speaking, thinking within the first epoch. Writing to be taught before reading because more active. Etheric forces freed from body at change of teeth; until then soul revealed in body. After this teaching in pictures needed to develop etheric. Astral (within etheric) works musically. Between 9th and 10th years the ego becomes conscious, and teaching of outer world can begin with plants. Plant never to be divorced from earth. The right treatment of the soil. Abstractions of modern thought in connection with speed of sound. Working of subconscious in child. Animals do not belong to earth, like plants, but are exaggerations of human form. Art for the etheric, music for the astral. The two combined manifest in Eurythmy, which must supplement Gymnastics. History and Geography to be taught pictorially till twelfth year, when child first understands causation. Explanation of child's so-called "animism". Danger of making all subjects "visual". Need for children to assimilate living concepts that grow. Dead concepts and sclerosis.

Lecture V ... ... Page 92

Importance of Teacher's Conference in Waldorf School. Insight needed to determine whether a talent is healthy or unhealthy. The supersensible is revealed in physical body of child, clairvoyance not needed. Example of a late developer. Hamerling's difficulty with the German language. Special class for children whose physical body does not release the spiritual. Medical knowledge for teachers. Steiner's own experience with hydrocephalic boy. Difference of classes where boys or girls predominate. Reciprocal feeling between teachers and children. The "main lesson" method and versatility of the teachers. Promise in the rascal. Goodness may be due to illness. Punishment. Qualifications for teachers. A unified educational ideal described. Contrast in parallel classes in Waldorf School. Behaviour of children at an inspection.

Lecture VI ... ... Page 111

Meetings of parents and teachers. Teachers should visit parents. Confidence of child in teacher begins to weaken between 9th and 10th year. How to strengthen it. Stories from the Gospels. Teacher is to read the book of the child. He should be inspired by anthroposophy but not teach it. Children should be kept in their own environment. Activities of children should be real. Children's sense of colour. Eurythmy should first be shown as an art, not as demonstrated by children. Abstract definitions to be avoided. Joy of understanding later in life what was learnt earlier. Experiencing good as pleasure and bad as displeasure in middle epoch is true basis of morality. 1st seven years, Gratitude: 2nd seven years, Love; 3rd seven years, Duty. Astral descends at puberty into physical and etheric, but is already working in twelfth year. Every man is bi-sexual, the male having female etheric body and vice versa.

Lecture VII ... ... Page 130

Anthroposophy sees spiritual world in concrete detail. It sees the spiritual in the physical and the physical as manifesting the spiritual. Treatment of pale child and over-red child (*a*) by medicine and (*b*) by education through right use of memory. The four temperaments. Advantage of grouping children by temperament. Teacher to embody and use all temperaments. Co-operation of school and home in matter of diet. Melancholic child to have more sugar, sanguine child less. Child of quick comprehension, who quickly forgets, may need to eat less potato. Sugar consumption in England and Russia. Effect of potato on intelligence in Europe. Deeper grasp with less detail changed to quick and more superficial intelligence. Coffee helps logical thoughts—for writers. Tea produces fleeting thoughts—for diplomats. Typical forms of carbohydrates, as seen through microscope, appear in astral body of potato consumers. Modern divorce of Art, Science and Religion. Supersensible sometimes allowed today in art (Bjornsen) and appears in strange places. Mystery Centres were places of unity of art, science and religion, which uniting man needs again today.

Lecture VIII ... ... Page 146

The four kingdoms of nature. The etheric body re-models physical in first seven years, but traces of the original model may survive. All teachers should practise sculpture, which helps in understanding etheric forces. Astral body fashioned out of music. Ancient architecture formed musically. From Greek age the mechanical and mathematical supplanted the musical. First Goetheanum again formed musically. Through astral man's body is a musical creation e.g. in breathing and blood circulation. Ratio of breath and pulse was basis of ancient poetry. The arm as formed by the musical scale. Singing and instruments to be taught in first school years. Intellectual, artistic and musical training needed for teachers to understand physical, etheric and astral. Ego reveals itself in speech. Differences of languages. Kopf and Testa. Example of form in speech. Observation needed by teacher, not intellect. The class and the individual child. History. Personalities and description of customs from 10th to 12th years. Making time spatially visible. Arithmetic to start with the whole.

Lecture IX ... ... Page 161

Relation of teacher and pupil in ancient East. Waldorf Education is for the whole man. Greek education based on the *Gymnast*. Women today more mobile in thinking than men. Greek thinking illustrated. Roman education less universal and based on the *Rhetorician*. This education still found in the mediaeval seven liberal arts, and even into Jesuit training. Modern education since the Renaissance limited to the intellect and its representative figure is the *Professor*. A modern professor of "Eloquence" who taught only archaeology. Abstract ideas in Marx of which none saw the consequences. Modern finance impersonal and out of touch with reality. Story of Rothschild and the ambassador. Prime need of a teacher is not knowledge but the understanding of man. Modern education destroys significance of world. Needed—medical knowledge for teacher, educational knowledge for doctor.

Lecture X ... ... Page 176

Thanks to organiser of the course. Spiritual revelation in ancient Mysteries worked in practical life. The same principle in new forms is possible today and is found in Waldorf education. The situation of anthroposophy compared to the early Christianity of the catacombs. The fate of the gnosis—to be obliterated—must not befall anthroposophy. The founding of Eurythmy and of the anthroposophical medical and educational movements arose from human needs and human personalities. The founding of the Waldorf School by Emil Molt coincided with a moment of freedom. Religious teaching in the Waldorf School. Its financial difficulties. It must be nurtured by love. Request by the top class in the school for an anthroposophical university. The problem of matriculation interfering with the curriculum dealt with by adding a 13th class. Progress or retrogression in civilisation depends on education. Waldorf education can show how anthroposophy works out of life.

LECTURE I*

ARNHEIM, 17 July, 1924

For quite a number of years now Education has been one of those branches of civilised, cultural activity which we foster within the Anthroposophical Movement, and, as will appear from these lectures, we may perhaps just in this sphere look back with a certain satisfaction on what we have been able to do. Our schools have existed only a few years, so I cannot speak of an achievement, but only of the beginning of something which, even outside the Anthroposophical Movement, has already made a certain impression on circles interested in the spiritual life of the cultural world of today. Looking back on our educational activity it gives me real joy, particularly here in Holland, where many years ago I had the opportunity of lecturing on subjects connected with anthroposophical spiritual science, to speak once more on this closely related theme.

Anthroposophical education and teaching is based on that knowledge of man which is only to be gained on the basis of spiritual science; it works out of a knowledge of the whole human being, body, soul and spirit. At first such a statement may be regarded as obvious. It will be said that of course the whole man must be taken into consideration when it is a question of educational practice, of education as an art; that neither should the spiritual be neglected in favour of the physical, nor the physical in favour of the spiritual. But it will very soon be seen how the matter stands when we become aware of the practical results which ensue when any branch of human activity is based on anthroposophical spiritual science. Here in Holland, in the Hague, a small school has been

* Dr. Steiner began his lecture by thanking Dr. Zeylmans van Emmichoven and those who arranged the course.

founded on the basis of an anthroposophical knowledge of man, a daughter school, if I may call it so, of our Waldorf School in Stuttgart. And I believe that whoever gets to know such a school, whether from merely hearing about the way it is run, or through a more intimate knowledge, will find in the actual way it deals with teaching and education, something arising from its anthroposophical foundation which differs essentially from the usual run of schools in our present civilisation. The reason for this is that wherever we look today we find a gulf between what people think, or devise theoretically, and what they actually carry out in practice. For in our present civilisation theory and practice have become two widely separated spheres. However paradoxical it may sound, the separation may be observed, perhaps most of all in the most practical of all occupations in life, in the business world, in the economic sphere. Here all sorts of things are learnt theoretically. For instance, people think out details of administration in economic affairs. They form intentions. But these intentions cannot be carried out in actual practice. However carefully they are thought out, they do not meet the actual conditions of life. I should like to express myself still more clearly, so that we may understand one another. For example, a man who wishes to set up a business concern thinks out some sort of business project. He thinks over all that is connected with this business and organises it according to his intentions.

His theories and abstract thoughts are then put into effect, but, when actually carried out, they everywhere come up against reality. Certainly things are done, thought-out ideas are even put into practice, but these thoughts do not fit into real life. In actual fact something is carried over into real life which does not correspond with what is real. Now a business that is conducted in this way can continue for some time and its inaugurator will consider himself to be a tremendously practical fellow. For whoever goes into business and from the outset has learnt absolutely nothing outside customary practice will consider himself a "practical" man.

Today we can hear how really practical people speak about such a theorist. He enters into business life and with a heavy hand introduces his thought-out ideas. If sufficient capital is available, he may even be able to carry on for a time. after a while, however, the concern collapses, or it may be absorbed into some more established business. Usually when this happens very little heed is paid to how much genuine, vital effort has been wasted, how many lives ruined, how many people injured or impaired in their way of life. It has come about solely because something has been thought out—thought out by a so-called "practical" man. In such a case however the person in question is not practical through his insight but by the use of his elbows. He has introduced something into reality without considering the conditions of reality.

Few people notice it, but this kind of thing has become rampant in the cultural life of today. At the present time the only sphere where such things are understood, where it is recognised that such a procedure does not work, is in the application of mechanical natural science to life. When the decision is made to build a bridge it is essential to make use of a knowledge of mechanics to ensure that the bridge will stand up to what is required of it; otherwise the first train that passes over it will be plunged into the water. Such things have already happened, and even at the present time we have seen the results of faulty mechanical construction. Speaking generally, however, this sphere is the only one in practical life in which it can be stated unequivocally that the conditions of reality have or have not been foreseen.

If we take the sphere of medicine we shall see at once that it is not so evident whether or not the conditions of reality have been taken into account. Here too the procedure is the same; something is thought out theoretically and then applied as a means of healing. Whether in this case there has been a cure, whether it was somebody's destiny to die, or whether perhaps he has been "cured to death", this indeed is difficult to perceive. The bridge collapses when there are faults in its construction; but whether the sick person gets worse, whether he has been cured by the treatment, or has died of it, is not so easy to discover.

In the same way, in the sphere of education it is not always possible to see whether the growing child is being educated in accordance with his needs, or whether fanciful methods are being used which can certainly be worked out by experimental psychology. In this latter case the child is examined by external means and the following questions arise : what sort of memory has he, what are his intellectual capacities, his ability to form judgments and so on? Educational aims are frequently found in this way. But how are they carried into life? They sit firmly in the head, that is where they are. In his head the teacher knows that a child must be taught arithmetic like this, geography like that, and so it goes on. Now the intentions are to be put into practice. The teacher considers all he has learnt, and remembers that according to the precepts of scientific educational method he must set about things in such and such a way. He is now faced with putting his knowledge into practice, he remembers these theoretical principles and applies them quite externally. Whoever has the gift for observing such things can experience how sometimes teachers who have thoroughly mastered educational theories, who can recount admirably everything they had to know for their examination, or had to learn in practice class-teaching, nevertheless remain utterly removed from life when they come face to face with the children they have to teach. What has happened to such a teacher is what, daily and hourly, we are forced to observe with sorrowing heart, the fact that people pass one another by in life, that they have no sense for getting to know one another. This is a common state of affairs. It is the fundamental evil which underlies all social disturbances which are so widespread in the cultural life of today : the lack of paying heed to others, the lack of interest which every man should have for others. In everyday civilised life we must perforce accept such a state of affairs; it is the destiny of modern humanity at the present time. But the peak of such aloofness is reached when the teacher of the child or the educator of the youth stands at a distance from his pupil, quite separated from him, and employs in a completely external way methods obtained by external science. We can see that the laws of mechanics have been wrongly applied when a bridge collapses, but wrong educational methods are not so obvious. A clear proof of the fact that human beings today are only at home when it comes to a mechanical way of thinking, which can always determine whether things have been rightly or wrongly thought out, and which has produced the most brilliant triumphs in the life of modern civilisation—a proof of this is that humanity today has confidence only in mechanical thought. And if this mechanical thinking is carried into education, if, for instance, the child is asked to write down disconnected words and then repeat them quickly, so that a record can be made of his power of assimilation, if this is the procedure in education it is a sign that there is no longer any natural gift for approaching the child himself. We experiment with the child because we can no longer approach his heart and soul.

In saying all this it might seem as though one had the inclination or desire only to criticise and reprove in a superior sort of way. It is of course always easier to criticise than to build something up constructively. But as a matter of fact what I have said does not arise out of any such inclination or desire; it arises out of a direct observation of life. This direct observation of life must proceed from something which is usually completely excluded from knowledge today. What sort of person must one be today if one wishes to pursue some calling based on knowledge—for instance on the knowledge of man? One must be objective! This is to be heard all over the place today, in every hole and corner. Of course one must be objective, but the question is whether or not this objectivity is based on a lack of paying due heed to what is essential in any particular situation.

Now for the most part people have the idea that love is far more subjective than anything else in life, and that it would be utterly impossible for anyone who loves to be objective. For this reason when knowledge is spoken about today love is never mentioned seriously. True, it is deemed fitting, when a young man is applying himself to acquire knowledge, to exhort him to do so with love, but this mostly happens when the whole way in which knowledge is presented is not at all likely to develop love in anybody But the essence of love, the giving of oneself to the world and its phenomena, is in any case not regarded as knowledge. Nevertheless for real life love is the greatest power of knowledge. And without this love it is utterly impossible to attain to a knowledge of man which could form the basis of a true art of education. Let us try to picture this love, and see how it can work in the special sphere of an education founded on a knowledge of man drawn from spiritual science, from anthroposophy.

The child is entrusted to us to be educated, to be taught. If our thinking in regard to education is founded on anthroposophy we do not represent the child to ourselves as something we must help to develop so that he approaches nearer and nearer to some social human ideal, or whatever it may be. For this human ideal can be completely abstract. And today such a human ideal has already become something which can assume as many forms as there are political, social and other parties. Human ideals change according to whether one swears by liberalism, conservatism, or by some other programme, and so the child is led slowly in some particular direction in order to become what is held to be right for mankind. This is carried to extreme lengths in present-day Russia. Generally speaking, however, it is more or less how people think today, though perhaps somewhat less radically.

This is no starting point for the teacher who wants to educate and teach on the basis of anthroposophy. He does not make an "idol" of his opinions. For an abstract picture of man, towards which the child shall be led, is an idol, it is in no sense a reality. The only reality which could exist in this field would be at most if the teacher were to consider himself as an ideal and were to say that every child must become like him. Then one would at least have touched on some sort of reality, but the absurdity of saying such a thing would at once be obvious.

What we really have before us in this young child is a being who has not yet begun his physical existence, but has brought down his spirit and soul from pre-earthly worlds, and has plunged into a physical body bestowed on him by parents and ancestors. We look upon this child as he lies there before us in the first days of his life with indeterminate features and with unorganised, undirected movements. We follow day by day, week by week how the features grow more and more defined, and become the expression of what is working to the surface from the inner life of soul. We observe further how the whole life and movements of the child become more consequent and directed, how something of the nature of spirit and soul is working its way to the surface from the inmost depths of his being. Then, filled with holy awe and reverence, we ask: "What is it that is here working its way to the surface?" And so with heart and mind we are led back to the human being himself, when as soul and spirit he dwelt in the soul-spiritual pre-earthly world from which he has descended into the physical world, and we say: "Little child, now that you have entered through birth into earthly existence you are among human beings, but previously you were among spiritual, divine beings." What once lived among spiritual-divine beings has descended in order to live among men. We see the divine made manifest in the child. We feel as though standing before an altar. There is however one difference. In religious communities it is customary for human beings to bring their sacrificial offerings to the altars, so that these offerings may ascend into the spiritual world; now we feel ourselves standing as it were before an altar turned the other way; now the gods allow their grace to stream down in the form of divine-spiritual beings, so that these beings, acting as messengers of the gods, may unfold what is essentially human on the altar of physical life. We behold in every child the unfolding of cosmic laws of a divine-spiritual nature; we see how God creates in the world. In its highest, most significant form this is revealed in the child. Hence every single child becomes for us a sacred riddle, for every single child embodies this great question—not, how is he to be educated so that he approaches some "idol" which has been thought out.—But, how shall we foster what the gods have sent down to us into the earthly world. We learn to know ourselves as helpers of the divine-spiritual world, and above all we learn to ask : What may be the result if we approach education with this attitude of mind?

Education in the true sense proceeds out of just such an attitude. What matters is that we should develop our education and teaching on the basis of such thoughts as these. Knowledge of man can only be won if love for mankind—in this case love for the child—becomes the mainspring of our work. If this is so, then the teacher's calling becomes a priestly calling, for then the educator becomes the steward of what it is the will of the gods to carry out with man.

Here again it might appear as though something obvious is being said in rather different words. But it is not so. As a matter of fact in today's unsocial world-order, which only wears an outer semblance of being social, the very opposite occurs. Educationists pursue an "idol" for mankind, not seeing themselves as nurturers of something they must first learn to know when actually face to face with the child.

An attitude of mind such as I have described cannot work in an abstract way, it must work spiritually, while always keeping the practical in view. Such an attitude however can never be acquired by accepting theories quite unrelated and alien to life, it can only be gained if one has a feeling, a sense for every expression of life, and can enter with love into all its manifestations.

Today there is a great deal of talk about educational reform. Since the war there has been talk of a revolution in education. We have experienced this. Every possible approach to a new education is thought out, and pretty well everybody is concerned in some way or other with how this reform is to be brought about. Either one approaches some institution about to be founded with one's proposals or at the very least one suggests this or that as one's idea of how education should take shape. And so it goes on. There is a great deal of talk about methods of education; but do you see what kind of impression all this makes when one surveys, quite without prejudice, what the various societies for the reform of education, down to the most radical, put forward today in their educational programmes? I do not know whether many people take into account what kind of impression is made when one is faced with so many programmes issuing from associations and societies for educational reform. One gets the impression : Good heavens, how clever people are today! For indeed everything which comes about like this is frightfully clever. I do not mean this ironically, but quite seriously. There has never been a time when there was so much cleverness as there is in our era.

There we have it, all set out. *Paragraph 1.* How shall we educate so that the forces of the child may be developed naturally? *Paragraph 2 . . . Paragraph 3 . . .* and so on. People today of any profession or occupation, and of any social class can sit down together and work out such programmes; everything we get in this way in paragraphs 1 to 30 will be delightfully clever, for today one knows just how to formulate everything theoretically. People have never been so skilful in formulating things as they are today. Then such a programme, a number of programmes can be submitted to a committee or to Parliament. This again is very clever. Now something may perhaps be deleted or added according to party opinion, and something extremely clever emerges, even if at times strongly coloured by "party". Nothing can be done with it, however, for all this is quite beside the point.

Waldorf School education never started off with such a programme. I have no wish to boast, but naturally, had this been our purpose, we could also have produced some kind of programme no less clever than those of many an association for educational reform. The fact that we should have to reckon with reality might perhaps prove a hindrance and then the result would be more stupid. With us however there was never any question of a programme. From the outset we were never interested in principles of educational method which might later on be somehow incorporated in a legalised educational system. What did interest us was reality, absolute true reality. What was this reality? To begin with here were children, a number of child-individualities with varying characteristics. One had to learn what these were, one had to get to know what was inherent in these children, what they had brought down with them, what was expressed through their physical bodies. First and foremost then there were the children. And then there were teachers. You can stand up as strongly as you like for the principle that the child must be educated in accordance with his individuality—that stands in all the programmes of reform—but nothing whatever will come of it. For on the other hand, besides the children, there are a number of teachers, and the point is to know what these teachers can accomplish in relation to these children. The school must be run in such a way that one does not set up an abstract ideal, but allows the school to develop out of the teachers and out of the pupils. And these teachers and pupils are not present in an abstract kind of way, but are quite concrete, individual human beings. That is the gist of the matter. Then we are led by virtue of necessity to build up a true education based on a real knowledge of man. We cease to be theoretical and become practical in every detail.

Waldorf School education, the first manifestation of an education based on anthroposophy, is actually the practice of education as an art, and is therefore able to give only indications of what can be done in this or that case. We have no great interest in general theories, but so much the greater is our interest in impulses coming from anthroposophy which can give us a true knowledge of man, beginning, as here of course it must do, with the child. But today our crude observation completely ignores what is most characteristic in the progressive stages of life. I would say that some measure of inspiration must be drawn from spiritual science if today we are to develop a right sense for what should be brought to the child.

At the present time people know extraordinarily little about man and mankind. They imagine that our present state of existence is the same as it was in the 14th, 15th and 16th centuries, and indeed as it has always been. They picture the ancient Greeks and the ancient Egyptians as being very similar to the man of today. And if we go back still further, according to the views of present-day natural science, history becomes enveloped in mist until those beings emerge which are half ape, half man. No interest is taken, however, in penetrating into the great differences which exist between the historical and pre-historical epochs of mankind.

Let us study the human being as he appears to us today, beginning with the child up to the change of teeth. We see quite clearly that his physical development runs parallel with his development of soul and spirit. Everything that manifests as soul and spirit has its exact counterpart in the physical—both appear together, both develop out of the child together. Then, when the child has come through the change of teeth, we see how the soul is already freeing itself from the body. On the one side we shall be able to follow a development of soul and spirit in the child, and on the other side his physical development. The two sides however are not as yet clearly separated. If we continue to follow the development further into the time between puberty and about the 21st year the separation becomes much more defined and then when we come to the 27th or 28th year—speaking now of present-day humanity—nothing more can be seen of the way in which the soul-spiritual is connected with the physical body. What a man does at this age can be perceived on the one hand in the soul-spiritual life and on the other hand in the physical life, but the two cannot be brought into any sort of connection. At the end of the twenties, man in his soul and spirit has separated himself completely from what is physical, and so it goes on up to the end of his life.

Yet it was not always so. One only believes it to have been so. Spiritual science, studied anthroposophically, shows us clearly and distinctly that what we see in the child today, at the present stage of human evolution—namely, that in his being of soul and spirit the child is completely dependent on his physical bodily nature and his physical bodily nature is completely dependent on his being of soul and spirit—this condition persisted right on into extreme old age—a fact that has simply not been noticed. If we go very far back into those times which gave rise to the conception of the patriarchs and ask ourselves what kind of a man such a patriarch really was, the answer must be somewhat as follows : Such a man, in growing old, changed in respect of his bodily nature, but right into extreme old age he continued to feel as only quite young people can feel today. Even in old age he felt his being of soul and spirit to be dependent on his physical body.

Today we no longer feel our physical body to be dependent upon what we think and feel. A dependence of this kind was however felt in the more ancient epochs of civilisation. But people also felt after a certain age of life that their bones became harder and their muscles contained certain foreign substances which brought about a sclerotic condition. They felt the waning of their life forces, but they also felt with this physical decline an increase of spiritual forces, actually brought about by the breaking up of the physical. "The soul is becoming free from the physical body". So they said when this process of physical decline began. At the age of the patriarchs, when the body was already breaking up, the soul was most able to wrest itself free from the body, so that it was no longer within it. This is why people looked up to the patriarchs with such devotion and reverence, saying : "O, how will it be with me one day, when I am so old ? For in old age one can know things, understand things, penetrate into the heart of things in a way that I cannot do now, because I am still building up my physical body." At that time man could still look into a world order that was both physical and spiritual. This however was in a very remote past. Then came a time when man felt this interdependence of the physical and the soul-spiritual only until about the 50th year. The Greek age followed. What gives the Greek epoch its special value rests on the fact that the Greeks were still able to feel the harmony between the soul-spiritual and the physical-bodily. The Greek still felt this harmony until the 30th or 40th year. He still experienced in the circulation of the blood what brought the soul into a unity with the physical. The wonderful culture and art of the Greeks was founded on this unity, which transformed everything theoretical into art, and at the same time enfilled art with wisdom.

In those times the sculptor worked in such a way that he needed no model, for in his own organisation he was aware of the forces permeating the arm or the leg, giving them their form. This was learned, for instance, in the festival games; but today when such games are imitated they have no meaning whatever.

If however we have such a sense for the development of mankind then we know what has actually taken place in human evolution. We know too that today we only have a parallelism between the physical-bodily and the soul-spiritual until about the 27th or 28th year, to give a quite exact description. (Most people observe this parallelism only up to the age of puberty.) And so we know how the divine-spiritual springs up and grows out of the developing human being. Then we feel the necessary reverence for our task of developing what comes to meet us in the child, that is to say, of developing what is *given* to us and not developing those abstract ideas that have been thought out.

Thus our thoughts are directed to a knowledge of man based on what is individual in the soul. And if we have absorbed such universal, great historical aspects, we shall also be able to approach every educational task in an appropriate manner. Then quite another life will be brought into the class when the teacher enters it, for he will carry the world into it, the physical world and the world of soul and spirit. Then he will be surrounded by an atmosphere of reality, of a real and actual conception of the world, not one which is merely thought out and intellectual. Then he will be surrounded by a world imbued with feeling. Now if we consider what has just been put forward we shall realise a remarkable fact. We shall see that we are founding an education which, by degrees, will come to represent in many respects the very opposite of the characteristic impulse in education at the present time. All manner of humorists with some aptitude for caricature often choose the so-called "schoolmaster" as an object which can serve their purpose well and on whom they can let loose their derision. Well, if a schoolmaster is endowed with the necessary humour he can turn the tables on those who have caricatured him before the world. But the real point is something altogether different; for if the teacher, versed in present-day educational methods, carries these into school with him, and has therefore no means of learning to know the child, while nevertheless having to deal with the child, how can he be anything other than a stranger to the world? With the school system as it is today, he cannot become anything else; he is torn right out of the world. So we are faced with a truly remarkable situation. Teachers who are strangers to the world are expected to train human beings so that they may get on and prosper in the world.

Let us imagine however that the things about which we have been speaking today become an accepted point of view. Then the relation of the teacher to the children is such that in each individual child a whole world is revealed to him, and not only a human world, but a divine-spiritual world manifested on earth. In other words the teacher perceives as many aspects of the world as he has children in his charge. Through every child he looks into the wide world. His education becomes art. It is imbued with the consciousness that what is done has a direct effect on the evolution of the world. Teaching in the sense meant here leads the teacher, in his task of educating, of developing human beings, to a lofty conception of the world. Such a teacher is one who becomes able to play a leading part in the great questions that face civilisation. The pupil will never outgrow such a teacher, as is so often the case today. The following situation may arise in a school. Let us suppose that the teacher has to educate according to some idea, some picture of man which he can set before himself. Let us think that he might have 30 children in his class, and among these, led by destiny, were two, who in their inborn capacity, were far more gifted than the teacher himself. What would he want to do in such a case? He would want to form them in accordance with his educational ideal; nothing else would be possible. But how does this work out? Reality does not permit it, and the pupils then outgrow their teacher.

If on the other hand we educate in accordance with reality, if we foster all that manifests in the child as qualities of soul and spirit, we are in the same situation as the gardener is in relation to his plants. Do you think that the gardener knows all these secrets of the plants which he tends? O, these plants contain many, many more secrets than the gardener understands; but he can tend them, and perhaps succeed best in caring for those which he does not yet know. His knowledge rests on practical experience, he has "green fingers". In the same way it is possible for a teacher who practises an art of education based on reality to stand as educator before children who have genius, even though he himself is certainly no genius. For he knows that he has not to lead his pupils towards some abstract ideal, but that in the child the Divine is working in man, is working right through his physical-bodily nature. If the teacher has this attitude of mind he can actually achieve what has just been said. He achieves it by an outpouring love which permeates his work as educator. It is his attitude of mind which is so essential.

With these words, offered as a kind of greeting, I wanted to give you today some idea of what is to be the content of this course of lectures. They will deal with the educational value of a knowledge of man and the cultural value of education.

LECTURE II

Arnheim, 18th July, 1924

In this course of lectures I want in the first place to speak about the way in which the art of education can be furthered and enriched by an understanding of man. I shall therefore approach the subject in the way I indicated in my introductory lecture, when I tried to show how anthroposophy can be a practical help in gaining a true knowledge of man, not merely a knowledge of the child, but a knowledge of the whole human being. I showed how anthroposophy, just because it has an all-embracing knowledge of the whole human being—that is to say a knowledge of the whole of human life from birth to death, in so far as this takes place on earth—how just because of this it can point out in a right way what is essential for the education and instruction of the child.

It is very easy to think that a child can be educated and taught if one observes only what takes place in childhood and youth; but this is not enough. On the contrary, just as with the plant, if you introduce some substance into the growing shoot its effect will be shown in the blossom or the fruit, so it is with human life. The effect of what is implanted into the child in his earliest years, or is drawn out of him during those years, will sometimes appear in the latest years of life; and often it is not realised that, when at about the age of 50 someone develops an illness or infirmity, the cause lies in a wrong education or a wrong method of teaching in the 7th or 8th year. What one usually does today is to study the child—even if this is done in a less external way than I described yesterday— in order to discover how best to help him. This is not enough. So today I should like to lay certain foundations, on the basis of which I shall proceed to show how the whole of human life can be observed by means of spiritual science.

I said yesterday that man should be observed as a being consisting of body, soul and spirit, and in yesterday's public lecture I gave some indication of how it is the supersensible in man, the higher man within man, that is enduring, that continues from birth until death, while the substances of the external physical body are always changing. It is therefore essential to learn to know human life in such a way that one perceives what is taking place on earth as a development of the pre-earthly life. We have not only those soul qualities within us that had their beginning at birth or at conception, but we bear within us pre-earthly qualities of soul, indeed, we bear within us the results of past earthly lives. All this lives and works and weaves within us, and during earthly life we have to prepare what will then pass through the gate of death and live again after death beyond the earth, in the world of soul and spirit. We must therefore understand how the super-earthly works into earthly life, for it is also present between birth and death. It works, only in a hidden way, in what is of a bodily nature, and one does not understand the body if one has no understanding of the spiritual forces active within it.

Let us now proceed to study further what I have just indicated. We can do so by taking concrete examples. An approach to the knowledge of man is contained in anthroposophical literature, for instance in my book *Theosophy*, in *An Outline of Occult Science* or in *Knowledge of the Higher Worlds*. Let us start from what can lead to a real, concrete knowledge of man by taking as a foundation what anthroposophy has to say in general about man and the world. There are two examples which I should like to put before you, two personalities who are certainly well known to you all. I choose them because for many years I made an intensive study of both of them. I am taking two men of genius; later on we shall come down to less gifted personalities. We shall then see that anthroposophy does not only speak in a general, abstract way, but is able to penetrate deeply into real human beings and is able to get to know them in such a way that knowledge of man is shown to be something which has reality in practical life. In choosing these two examples, Goethe and Schiller, and so making an indirect approach, I hope to show how a knowledge of man is acquired under the influence of Spiritual Science.

Let us look at Goethe and Schiller from an outward point of view, as they appeared during the course of their lives, but let us in each case study the whole personality. In Goethe we have an individuality who entered life in a remarkable way. He was born black, or rather dark blue. This shows how extraordinarily difficult it was for his soul-spiritual being to enter into physical incarnation. But once this had taken place, once Goethe had overcome the resistance of this physical body, he was entirely within it. On the one hand it is hard to imagine a more healthy nature than Goethe had as a boy. He was amazingly healthy. He was so healthy that his teachers found him quite difficult; but children who give no trouble are seldom those who enjoy the best health in later life. On the other hand, children who are rather a nuisance to their teachers are those who accomplish more in later life because they have more active, energetic natures. The understanding teacher will therefore be quite glad when the children keep a sharp eye on him. Goethe from his earliest childhood was very much inclined to do this, even in the literal sense of the word. He peeped at the fingers of someone playing the piano and then named one finger "Thumbkin", another "Pointerkin", and so on. But it was not only in this sense that he kept a sharp eye on his teachers. Even in his boyhood he was bright and wide-awake; and this at times gave them trouble. Later on in Leipzig Goethe went through a severe illness, but here we must bear in mind that certain hard experiences and some sowing of wild oats were necessary in order to bring about a lowering of his health to the point at which he could be attacked by the illness which he suffered at Leipzig. After this illness we see that Goethe throughout this whole life is a man of robust health, but one who possesses at the same time an extraordinary sensitivity. He reacts strongly to impressions of all kinds, but does not allow them to take hold of him and enter deeply into his organism. He does not suffer from heart trouble when he is deeply moved by some experience, but he feels any such experience intensely; and this sensitivity of soul goes with him throughout life. He suffers, but his suffering does not find expression in physical illness. This shows that his bodily health was exceptionally sound. Moreover, Goethe felt called upon to exercise restraint in his way of looking at things. He did not sink into a sort of hazy mysticism and say, as is so often said : "O, it is not a question of paying heed to the external physical form; that is of small importance. We must turn our gaze to what is spiritual!" On the contrary, to a man with Goethe's healthy outlook the spiritual and the physical are one. And he alone can understand such a personality who is able to behold the spiritual through the image of the physical.

Goethe was tall when he sat, and short when he stood. When he stood you could see that he had short legs.* This is an especially important characteristic for the observer who is able to regard man as a whole. Why had Goethe short legs? Short legs are the cause of a certain kind of walk. Goethe took short steps because the upper part of his body was heavy— heavy and long—and he placed his foot firmly on the ground. As teachers we must observe such things, so that we can study them in the children. Why is it that a person has short legs and a particularly big upper part of the body? It is the outward sign that such a person is able to bring to harmonious expression in the present earth life what he experienced in a previous life on earth. In this respect also Goethe was extraordinarily harmonious, for right into extreme old age he was able to develop everything that lay in his karma. Indeed he lived to be so old because he was able to bring to fruition the potential gifts with which karma had endowed him. After Goethe had left

* The German has the word Sitzgrösse for this condition.

the physical body, this body was still so beautiful that all who saw him in death were fulfilled with wonder. One has the impression that Goethe had experienced to the full his karmic potentialities; now nothing more is left, and he must begin afresh when again he enters into an earthly body under completely new conditions. All this is expressed in the particular formation of such a body as Goethe's, for the cause of what man brings with him as predisposition from an earlier incarnation is revealed for the most part in the formation of the head. Now Goethe from his youth up had a wonderfully beautiful Apollo head, from which only harmonious forces streamed down into his physical body. This body, however, burdened by the weight of its upper part and with too short legs was the cause of his special kind of walk which lasted throughout his life. The whole man was a wonderfully harmonious expression of karmic predisposition and karmic fulfilment. Every detail of Goethe's life illustrates this.

Such a personality, standing so harmoniously in life and becoming so old, must inevitably have outstanding experiences in his middle years. Goethe was born in 1749 and he died in 1832, so he lived to be 83 years old. He reached middle age, therefore, at about his 41st year in 1790. If we take these years between 1790 and 1800 we have the middle decade of his life. In this decade, before 1800, Goethe did indeed experience the most important events of his life. Before this time he was not able to bring his philosophical and scientific ideas, important as they were, to any very definite formulation. The *Metamorphosis of the Plants* was first published in 1790; everything connected with it belongs to this decade 1790–1800. In 1790 Goethe was so far from completing his Faust that he brought it out as a Fragment; he had no idea then that he would ever finish it. It was in this decade that under the influence of his friendship with Schiller he conceived the bold idea of continuing his Faust. The great scenes, the Prologue in Heaven among others, belong to this period. So in Goethe we have to do with an exceptionally harmonious life; with a life moreover that runs its quiet course, undisturbed by inner conflict, devoted freely and contemplatively to the outer world.

As a contrast let us look at the life of Schiller. From the outset Schiller is placed into a situation in life which shows a continual disharmony between his life of soul and spirit and his physical body. His head completely lacks the harmonious formation which we find in Goethe. He is even ugly, ugly in a way that does not hide his gifts, but nevertheless ugly. In spite of this a strong personality is shown in the way he holds himself, and this comes to expression in his features also, particularly in the formation of the nose. Schiller is not long-bodied; he has long legs. On the other hand everything that lies between the head and the limbs, in the region of the circulation and breathing is in his case definitely sick, poorly developed from birth, and he suffers throughout his life from cramps. To begin with there are long periods between the attacks, but later they become almost incessant. They become indeed so severe that he is unable to accept any invitation to a meal; but has to make it a condition—as for instance on one occasion when coming to Berlin—that he is invited for the whole day, so that he may be able to choose a time free from such pains. The cause of all this is an imperfect development of the circulatory and breathing systems.

The question therefore arises: What lies karmically, coming from a previous earthly life, in the case of a man who has to suffer in this way from cramping pains? Such pains, when they gain a hold in human life, point quite directly to a man's karma. If, with a sense of earnest scientific responsibility, one attempts to investigate these cramp phenomena from the standpoint of spiritual science, one always finds a definite karmic cause underlying them, the results of deeds, thoughts and feelings coming from an earlier life on earth. Now we have the man before us, and one of two things can happen. Either everything goes as harmoniously as with Goethe, so that one says to oneself: Here we have to do with Karma; here everything appears as the result of Karma. Or the opposite can also happen. Through special conditions which arise when a man descends out of the spiritual world into the physical, he comes into a situation in which he is not able fully to work through the burden of his karma.

Man comes down from the spiritual world with definite karmic predispositions; he bears these within him. Let us assume that *A* in the diagram represents a place, a definite point of time in the life of a man when he should be able in some way to realise, to fulfil his karma, but for some reason this does not happen. Then the fulfilment of his karma is interrupted and a certain time must pass when, as it were, his karma makes a pause; it has to be postponed until the next life on earth. And so it goes on. Again, at *B* there comes a place when he should be able to fulfil something of his karma; but once more he has to pause and again postpone this part of his karma until his next incarnation. Now when someone is obliged to interrupt his karma in this way pains of a cramping nature always make their appearance in the course of life. Such a person is unable fully to fashion and shape into his life what he always bears within him. Here we have something which shows the true character of spiritual science. It does not indulge in fantasy, neither does it talk in vague, general terms about the four members of man's being; physical body, etheric body, astral body and ego. On the contrary, it penetrates into real life, and is able to point out where the real spiritual causes lie for certain external occurrences. It knows how man represents *himself* in outer life. This knowledge is what true spiritual science must be able to achieve.

I was now faced with the question: In a life such as Schiller's, how does karma work as the shaper of the whole of life if, as in his case, conditions are such that karma cannot properly operate, so that he has to make continual efforts to achieve what he has the will to achieve? For

Goethe it was really comparatively easy to complete his great
works. For Schiller the act of creation is always very difficult.
He has, as it were, to attack his karma, and the way in
which he goes to the attack will only show its results in the
following earthly life. So one day I had to put to myself the
following question : What is the connection between such a
life as Schiller's and the more general conditions of life? If
one sets about answering such a question in a superficial way
nothing of any significance emerges, even with the help of
the investigations of spiritual science. Here one may not spin
a web of fantasy; one must observe. Nevertheless if one
approaches straight away the first object that presents itself
for observation, one will somehow go off on a side track. So
I considered the question in the following way : How does a
life take its course when karmic hindrances or other pre-
earthly conditions are present?

I then proceeded to study certain individuals in whom
something of this kind had already happened, and I will now
give such an example. I could give many similar examples,
but I will take one which I can describe quite exactly. I had
an acquaintance, a personality whom I knew very well indeed
in his present earthly life. I was able to establish that there
were no hindrances in his life connected with the fulfilment of
karma, but there were hindrances resulting from what had
taken place in his existence between death and a new birth,
that is in his supersensible life between the last earthly life and
the one in which I learned to know him. So in this case there
were not, as with Schiller, hindrances preventing the fulfilment
of karma, but hindrances in the way of bringing down into
the physical body what he had experienced between death and
a new birth in the supersensible world. In observing this man
one could see that he had experienced much of real significance between death and a new birth, but was not able to
give expression to this in life. He had entered into karmic
relationships with other people and had incarnated at a time
when it was not possible fully to realise on earth what he had,
as it were, piled up as the content of his inner soul experience

between death and conception. And what were the physical manifestations which appeared as the result of his not being able to realise what had been present in him in the supersensible world? These showed themselves through the fact that this personality was a stutterer; he had an impediment in his speech. And if one now takes a further step and investigates the causes at work in the soul which result in speech disturbances, then one always finds that there is some hindrance preventing what was experienced between death and a new birth in the supersensible world from being brought down through the body into the physical world. Now the question arises : How do matters stand in the case of such a personality who has very much in him brought about through his previous karma, but who has it all stored up in the existence between death and a new birth and, because he cannot bring it down becomes a stutterer? What sort of things are bound up with such a personality in his life here on earth?

Again and again one could say to oneself : This man has in him many great qualities that he has gained in pre-earthly life, but he cannot bring them down to earth. He was quite able to bring down what can be developed in the formation of the physical body up to the time of the change of teeth; he could even develop extremely well what takes place between the change of teeth and puberty. He then became a personality with outstanding literary and artistic ability, for he was able to form and fashion what can be developed between puberty and the 30th year of life. Now, however, there arose a deep concern in one versed in a true knowledge of man, a concern which may be expressed in the following question: How will it be with this personality when he enters his thirties and should then develop to an ever increasing degree the spiritual or consciousness soul in addition to the intellectual or mind soul? Anyone who has knowledge of these things feels the deepest concern in such a case, for he cannot think that the consciousness soul—which needs for its unfolding everything that arises in the head, perfect and complete—will be able to come to its full development. For with this personality the fact

that he stuttered showed that not everything in the region of
his head was in proper order. Now apart from stuttering this
man was as sound as a bell, except that in addition to the
stutter, (which showed that not everything was in order in the
head system) he suffered from a squint. This again was a sign
that he had not been able to bring down into the present
earthly life all that he had absorbed in the supersensible life
between death and a new birth. Now one day this man came
to me and said : "I have made up my mind to be operated on
for my squint." I was not in a position to do more than say,
"If I were you, I should not have it done." I did all I could
to dissuade him. I did not at that time see the whole situation
as clearly as I do today, for what I am telling you happened
more than 20 years ago. But I was greatly concerned about
this operation. Well, he did not follow my advice and the
operation took place. Now note what happened. Very soon
after the operation, which was extremely successful, as such
operations often are, he came to me in jubilant mood and
said, "Now I shall not squint any more." He was just a little
vain, as many distinguished people often are. But I was very
troubled; and only a few days later the man died, having just
completed his 30th year. The doctors diagnosed typhoid, but it
was not typhoid, he died of meningitis.

There is no need for the spiritual investigator to become
heartless when he considers such a life; on the contrary his
human sympathy is deepened thereby. But at the same time
he sees through life and comprehends it in its manifold aspects
and relationships. He perceives that what was experienced
spiritually between death and a new birth cannot be brought
down into the present life and that this comes to expression in
physical defects. Unless the right kind of education can inter-
vene, which was not possible in this case, life cannot be
extended beyond certain definite limits. Please do not believe
that I am asserting that anybody who squints must die at
30. Negative instances are never intended and it may well
be that something else enters karmically into life which enables
the person in question to live to a ripe old age. But in the case

we are considering there was cause for anxiety because of the demands made on the head, which resulted in squinting and stuttering, and the question arose : How can a man with an organisation of this kind live beyond the 35th year? It is at this point of time that one must look back on a person's karma, and then you will see immediately that it in no way followed that because somebody had a squint he must die at 30. For if we take a man who has so prepared himself in pre-earthly life that he has been able to absorb a great deal between death and a new birth, but is unable to bring down what he has received into physical life, and if we consider every aspect of his karma, we find that this particular person-ality might quite well have lived beyond the 35th year; but then, besides all other conditions, he would have had to bear within him the impulse leading to a spiritual conception of man and of the world. For this man had a natural disposition for spiritual things which one rarely meets; but in spite of this, because strong spiritual impulses inherent in him from previous earth lives were too one-sided, he could not approach the spiritual.

I assure you that I am in a position to speak about such a matter. I was very friendly with this man and was therefore well aware of the deep cleft that existed between my own conception of the world and his. From the intellectual stand-point we could understand one another very well; we could be on excellent terms in other ways, but it was not possible to speak to him about the things of the spirit. Thus because with his 35th year it would have been necessary for him to find his way to a spiritual life, if his potential gifts up to this age were to be realised on earth, and because he was not able to come to a spiritual life, he died when he did. It is of course perfectly possible to stutter and have a squint and yet continue one's life as an ordinary mortal. There is no need to be afraid of things which must be stated at times if one wishes to describe realities, and not waste one's breath in mere phrases. Moreover from this example you can see how observation, sharpened by spiritual insight, enables one to look deeply into human life.

And now let us return to Schiller. When we consider the life of Schiller two things strike us above all others, for they are quite remarkable. There exists an unfinished drama by Schiller, a mere sketch, called the *Malteser*. We see from the concept underlying this sketch that if Schiller had wished to complete this drama, he could only have done so as an initiate, as one who had experienced initiation. It could not have been done otherwise. Up to a certain degree at least he possessed the inner qualities necessary for initiation, but owing to other conditions of his karma these qualities could not get through; they were suppressed, cramped. There was a cramping of his soul life too which can be seen in the sketch of the *Malteser*. There are long powerful sentences which never manage to get to the full stop. What is in him cannot find its way out. Now it is interesting to observe that with Goethe, too, we have such unfinished sketches, but we see that in his case, whenever he left something unfinished, he did so because he was too easy-going to carry it further. He could have finished it. Only in extreme old age, when a certain condition of sclerosis had set in would this have been impossible for him. With Schiller however we have another picture. An iron will is present in him when he makes the effort to develop the *Malteser* but he cannot do it. He only gets as far as a slight sketch. For this drama, seen in its reality, contains what, since the time of the Crusades, has been preserved in the way of all kinds of occultism, mysticism, and initiation science. And Schiller sets to work on such a drama, for the completion of which he would have had to bear within him the experience of initiation. Truly a life's destiny which is deeply moving for one who is able to see behind these things and look into the real being of this man. And from the time it became known that Schiller had in mind to write a drama such as the *Malteser* there was a tremendous increase in the opposition to him in Germany. He was feared. People were afraid that in his drama he might betray all kinds of occult secrets.

The second work about which I wish to speak is the following. Schiller is unable to finish the *Malteser*; he cannot get on with it. He lets some time go by and writes all manner of things which are certainly worthy of admiration, but which can also be admired by so-called philistines. If he could have completed the *Malteser*, it would have been a drama calling for the attention of men with the most powerful and vigorous minds. But he had to put it aside.

After a while he gets a new impulse which inspires his later work. He cannot think any more about the *Malteser*, but he begins to compose his *Demetrius*. This portrays a remarkable problem of destiny, the story of the false Demetrius who takes the place of another man. All the conflicting destinies which enter into the story as though emerging out of the most hidden causes, all the human emotions thereby aroused, would have had to be brought into this drama, if it were to be completed. Schiller sets to work on it with feverish activity. It became generally known—and people were still more afraid that things would be brought into the open which it was to their interest to keep hidden from the rest of mankind for some time yet.

And now certain things take place in the life of Schiller which, for anyone who understands them, cannot be accounted for on the grounds of a normal illness. We have a remarkable picture of this illness of Schiller's. Something tremendous happens—tremendous not only in regard to its greatness, but in regard to its shattering force. Schiller is taken ill while writing his *Demetrius*. On his sick bed in raging fever he continually repeats almost the whole of *Demetrius*. It seems as though some alien power is at work in Schiller, expressing itself through his body. There is of course no ground for accusing anyone. But, in spite of everything that has been written in this connection, one cannot do otherwise than come to the conclusion, from the whole picture of the illness, that in some way or another, even if in a quite occult way, something contributed to the rapid termination of Schiller's illness in his death. That people had some suspicion of this may be gathered from the fact that

Goethe, who could do nothing, but suspected much, dared not participate personally in any way during the last days of Schiller's life, not even after his death, although he felt this deeply. He dared not venture to make known the thoughts he bore within him.

With these remarks I only want to point out that for anyone able to see through such things Schiller was undoubtedly pre-destined to create works of a high spiritual order, but on account of inner and outer causes, inner and outer karmic reasons, it was all held back, dammed up, as it were, within him. I venture to say that for the spiritual investigator there is nothing of greater interest than to set himself the problem of studying what Schiller achieved in the last ten years of his life, from the *Aesthetic Letters* onwards, and then to follow the course of his life after death. A deep penetration into Schiller's soul after death reveals manifold inspirations coming to him from the spiritual world. Here we have the reason why Schiller had to die in his middle forties. His condition of cramp and his whole build, especially the ugly formation of his head, made it impossible for him to bring down into the physical body the content of his soul and spirit, deeply rooted as this was in spiritual existence.

When we bear such things in mind we must admit that the study of human life is deepened if we make use of what anthroposophy can give. We learn to look right into human life. In bringing these examples before you my sole purpose was to show how through anthroposophy one learns to contemplate the life of human beings. But let us now look at the matter as a whole. Can we not deepen our feeling and understanding for everything that is human simply by looking at a single human life in the way that we have done? If at a certain definite moment of life one can say to oneself : Thus it was with Schiller, thus with Goethe; thus it was with another young man—as I have told you—then, will not something be stirred in our souls which will teach us to look upon every child in a deeper way? Will not every human life become a sacred riddle to us? Shall we not learn to contemplate every human life, every human being, with much greater, much more inward attention? And can we not, just because a knowledge of man has been inscribed in this way into our souls, deepen within us a love of mankind? Can we not with this human love, deepened by a study of man which gives such profundity to the most inward, sacred riddle of life—can we not, with this love, enter rightly upon the task of education when life itself has become so sacred to us? Will not the teacher's task be transformed from mere ideological phrases or dream-like mysticism into a truly priestly calling ready for its task when Divine Grace sends human beings down into earthly life?

Everything depends on the development of such feelings. The essential thing about anthroposophy is not mere theoretical teaching, so that we know that man consists of physical body, etheric body, astral body and ego; that there is a law of karma, of reincarnation and so on. People can be very clever, they can know everything; but they are not anthroposophists in the true sense of the word when they only know these things in an ordinary way, as they might know the content of a cookery book. What matters is that the life of human souls is quickened and deepened by the anthroposophical world conception and that one then learns to work and act out of a soul-life thus deepened and quickened.

This then is the first task to be undertaken in furthering an education based on anthroposophy. From the outset one should work in such a way that teachers and educators may become in the deepest sense "knowers of men", so that out of their own conviction, as a result of observing human beings in the right way, they approach the child with the love born out of this kind of thinking. It follows therefore that in a training course for teachers wishing to work in an anthroposophical sense the first approach is not to say : you should do it like this or like that, you should employ this or that educational knack, but the first thing is to awaken a true educational sense born out of a knowledge of man. If one has been successful in bringing this to the point of awakening in the teacher a real love of education then one can say that he is now ready to begin his work as an educator.

In education based on a knowledge of man, such for instance as the Waldorf School education, the first thing to be considered is not the imparting of rules, not the giving advice as to how one should educate, but the first thing is to hold Training Courses for Teachers in such a way that one finds the hearts of the teachers and so deepens these hearts that love for the child grows out of them. It is quite natural that every teacher believes that he can, as it were, impose this love on himself, but such an imposed human love can achieve nothing. Much good will may be behind it, but it can achieve nothing. The only human love which can achieve something is that which arises out of a deepened observation of individual cases.

If someone really wishes to develop an understanding of the essential principles of education based on a knowledge of man— whether he has already acquired a knowledge of spiritual science or whether, as can also happen, he has an instinctive understanding of these things—he will observe the child in such a way that he is faced with this question : What is the main trend of a child's development up to the time of the change of teeth? An intimate study of man will show that up to the change of teeth the child is a completely different being from what he becomes later on. A tremendous inner transformation takes place at this time, and there is another tremendous transformation at puberty. Just think what the change of teeth signifies for the growing child. It is only the outer sign for deep changes which are taking place in the whole human being, changes which occur only once, for only once do we get our second teeth, not every seven years. With the change of teeth the formative process taking place in the teeth comes to an end. From now on we have to keep our teeth for the rest of our lives. The most we can do is to have them stopped, or replaced by false ones, for we get no others out of our organism. Why is this? It is because with the change of teeth the organisation of the head is brought to a certain conclusion. If we are aware of this, if in each single case we ask ourselves : What actually is it that is brought to a conclusion with the change of teeth?—we are led, just at this point, to a comprehension of the whole human organisation, body, soul and spirit. And if—with our gaze deepened by a love gained through a knowledge of man such as I have described—we observe the child up to the change of teeth, we shall see that during these years he learns to walk, to speak and to think. These are the three most outstanding faculties to be developed up to the change of teeth.

Walking entails more than just learning to walk. Walking is only one manifestation of what is actually taking place, for it involves learning to adapt oneself to the world through acquiring a sense of balance. Walking is only the crudest expression of this process. Before learning to walk the child is not exposed to the necessity of finding his equilibrium in the world : now he learns to do this. How does it come about? It comes about through the fact that man is born with a head which requires a quite definite position in regard to the forces of balance. The secret of the human head is shown very clearly in the physical body. You must bear in mind that an average human brain weighs between 1,200 and 1,500 grammes. Now if such a weight as this were to press on the delicate veins which lie at the base of the brain they would be crushed immediately. This is prevented by the fact that this heavy brain floats in the cerebral fluid that fills our head. You will doubtless remember from your studies in physics that when a body floats in a fluid it loses as much of its weight as the weight of the fluid it displaces. If you apply this to the brain you will discover that our brain presses on its base with a weight of about 20 grammes only; the rest of the weight is lost in the cerebral fluid. Thus at birth man's brain has to be so placed that its weight can be brought into proper proportion in regard to the displaced cerebral fluid. This adjustment is made when we raise ourselves from the crawling to the upright posture. The position of the head must now be brought into relationship with the rest of the organism. Walking and using the hands make it necessary for the head to be brought into a definite position. Man's sense of balance proceeds from the head.

Let us go further. At birth man's head is relatively highly organised, for up to a point it is already formed in the embryo, although it is not fully developed until the change of teeth. What however is first established during the time up to the change of teeth, what then receives its special outer organisation, is the rhythmic system of man. If people would only observe physical physiological processes more closely they would see how important the establishing of the circulatory and breathing systems is for the first seven years. They would recognise how here above all great damage can be done if the bodily life of the child does not develop in the right way. One must therefore reckon with the fact that in these first years of life something is at work which is only now establishing its own laws in the circulatory and breathing systems. The child feels unconsciously how his life forces are working in his circulation and breathing. And just as a physical organ, the brain, must bring about a state of balance, so must the soul in the first years of life play its part in the development of the breathing and circulatory systems. The physical body must be active in bringing about a state of balance proceeding from the head. The soul, in that it is rightly organised for this purpose, must be active in the changes that take place in the circulation and breathing. And just as the upright carriage and learning to use the hands and arms are connected with what comes to expression in the brain, so the way in which speech develops in man is connected with the systems of circulation and breathing. Through learning to speak man establishes a relationship with his circulation and breathing, just as he establishes a relationship between walking and grasping and the forces of the head by learning to hold the latter in such a way that the brain loses the right amount of weight. If you train yourself to perceive these relationships and then you meet someone with a clear, high-pitched voice particularly well-suited to the recitation of hymns or odes, or even to declamatory moral harangues, you may be sure that this is connected with special conditions of the circulatory system. Or again if you meet someone with a rough, harsh voice, with a voice like the beating together of sheets of brass and tin, you may be sure that this too is connected with the breathing or circulatory systems. But there is more to it than this. When one learns to listen to a child's voice, whether it be harmonious and pleasant, or harsh and discordant, and when one knows that this is connected with movements of the lungs and the circulation of the blood, movements inwardly vibrating through the whole man, right into the fingers and toes, then one knows that what is expressed through speech is imbued with qualities of soul. And now something in the nature of a higher man, so to say, makes its appearance, something which finds its expression in this picture relating speech with the physical processes of circulation and breathing. Taking our start from this point it is possible to look up and see into the pre-natal life of man which is subject to those conditions which we have made our own between death and a new birth. What a man has experienced in pre-earthly conditions plays in here, and so we learn that if we are to comprehend the being of man by means of true human understanding and knowledge we must train our ear to a spiritual hearing and listen to the voices of children. We can then know how to help a child whose strident voice betrays the fact that there is some kind of obstruction in his karma and we can do something to free him from such karmic hindrances.

From all this we can see what is necessary for education. It is nothing less than a knowledge of man; not merely the sort of knowledge that says : "This is a gifted personality, this is a good fellow, this is a bad one", but the kind of knowledge that follows up what lies in the human being, follows up for instance what is spiritually present in speech and traces this right down into the physical body, so that one is not faced with an abstract spirituality but with a spirituality which comes to expression in the physical image of man. Then, as a teacher, you can set to work in such a way that you take into consideration both spirit and body and are thus able to help the physical provide a right foundation for the spirit. And further, if you observe a child from behind and see that he has short legs, so that the upper part of the body is too heavy a burden and his tread is consequently also heavy, you will know, if you have acquired the right way of looking at these things, that here the former earthly life is speaking, here karma is speaking. Or, for instance if you observe someone who walks in the same way as the German philosopher Johann Gottlieb Fichte, who always walked with his heels well down first, and even when he spoke did so in such a way that the words came out, as it were "heels first", then you will see in such a man another expression of karma.

In this way we learn to recognise karma in the child through observation based on spiritual science. This is something of the greatest importance which we must look into and understand. Our one and only help as teachers is that we learn to observe human beings, to observe the bodies of the children, the souls of the children and the spirits of the children. In this way a knowledge of man must make itself felt in the sphere of education, but it must be a knowledge which is deepened in soul and spirit.

With this lecture I wanted to call up a picture, to give an idea of what we are trying to achieve in education, and what can arise in the way of practical educational results from what many people consider to be highly unpractical, what they look upon as being merely fantastic day-dreaming.

LECTURE III

Arnheim, 19th July, 1924

You will have gathered from the remarks I have made during the last two days that there is a fundamental change in the inner constitution of the human being at every single stage of his life. Today, certainly, modern psychologists and physiologists also take this into account. They too reckon with these changes which take place in the course of life, firstly up to the change of teeth, then up to puberty, and again from puberty into the twenties. But these differences are more profound than can be discovered by means of the methods of observation customary today, which do not reach far enough, however excellent they may be. We must take a further step and examine these differences from aspects demanded by spiritual science. You will hear many things that are already familiar to you, but you must now enter more deeply into them. Even when the child enters this world from the embryo condition, that is, to take an external characteristic, when he adapts himself to the outer process of breathing, even then, physiologically speaking, he is not yet received directly by the outer world, for he takes the natural nourishment of the mother's milk. He is not nourished as yet by what comes from the outer world, but by what comes from the same source as the child himself. Now today people study the substances they meet with in the world more or less according to their external, chemical, physical properties only and do not consider the finer attributes which they possess through their spiritual content. Nowadays everything is considered in this way. Such methods are not to be condemned; on the contrary they should be recognised as justified. Nevertheless because the time came when man was concerned only with the outer aspects of things, aspects which could not be so regarded in earlier civilisations, he has now reached a point of extreme externalisation. If I may make a comparison, things are observed today in some such way as this. We say : I look upon death, upon dying; plants die, animals die, human beings die. But surely the question arises as to whether dying, the passing away of the various forms of life with which we come in contact, is in all three kinds of living beings the same process, or whether this only appears outwardly to be so. We can make use of the following comparisons : If I have a knife there is a real difference whether I cut my food with it, or whether I use it for shaving. In each case it is a knife, but the properties of "knife" must be further differentiated. Such differentiation is in many cases not made today. No differentiation is made between the dying of a plant, an animal or a man.

We meet the same thing in other domains too. There are people who in a certain way want to be philosophers of nature, and because they aim at being idealistic, even spiritual, they assert that plants may well have a soul; and they try to discover in an external way those characteristics of plants which seem to indicate that they have certain soul qualities. They make a study of those plants which, when they are approached by insects, tend to open their petals. The insect is caught, for it is attracted by the scent of what is in the plant. Such a plant is the Venus Flytrap. It closes its petals with a snap and the insect is trapped. This is considered to be a sort of soul quality in the plant. Well, but I know something else which works in the same way. It is to be found in all sorts of places. The mouse, when it comes near, feels attracted by the smell of a dainty morsel; it begins to nibble, and—hey presto ! snap goes the mousetrap. If one were to make use of the same thought process as in the case of a plant, one might say : the mousetrap has a soul.

This kind of thinking, however, although quite legitimate under certain conditions never leads to conclusions of any depth, but remains more or less on the surface. If we wish to gain a true knowledge of man we must penetrate into the very depths of human nature. It must be possible for us to look in a completely unprejudiced way at things which appear paradox-ical vis-à-vis external methods of observation. Moreover it is very necessary to take into consideration everything which, taken together, makes up the entire human organisation.

In man we have, to begin with, the actual physical organism which he has in common with all earthly beings and parti-cularly with the mineral kingdom. In man, however, we have clearly to distinguish between his physical organism and his etheric organism. The latter he has in common only with the plant world, not with the minerals. But a being endowed only with an etheric organism could never experience feeling, never attain to an inner consciousness. For this again man has his astral organism, which he has in common with the animal world. It might appear that this is an external organisation, but in the course of these lectures we shall see how inward it can be. In addition to this man still has his ego-organisation, which is not to be found in the animal world and which he alone possesses among earthly beings. What we are here considering is in no sense merely an external, intellectual pattern; moreover, in speaking, for instance, of an etheric or life-body, this has no connection whatever with what an out-moded natural science once called "life-force", "vital-force" and so on. On the con-trary, it is the result of observation. If, for instance, we study the child up to the age of the change of teeth, we see that his development is primarily dependent on his physical organism. The physical organism must gradually adapt itself to the outer world, but this cannot take place all at once, not even if considered in the crudest physical sense. This physical body, just because it contains what the human being has brought with him out of the spiritual world in which he lived in pre-earthly existence, cannot forthwith assimilate the substances of the outer world, but must receive them specially prepared in the mother's milk. The child must, so to say, remain closely con-nected with what is of like nature with himself. He must only gradually grow into the outer world. And the conclusion of this process of the physical organism growing into the outer world is indicated by the appearance of the second teeth at about the seventh year. At approximately this age the child's physical organism completes the process of growing into the world.

During this time, however, in which the organisation is chiefly concerned with the shaping and fashioning of the bony system, the child is only interested in certain things in the outer world, not in everything. He is only interested in what we might call gesture, everything that is related to movement. Now you must take into account that at first the child's consciousness is dream-like, shadowy; to begin with his perceptions are quite undefined, and only gradually do they light up and gain clarity. But fundamentally speaking the fact remains that during the time between birth and the change of teeth the child's perception adheres to everything in the nature of gesture and movement and does so to such an extent, that in the very moment when he perceives a movement he feels an inner urge to imitate it. There exists a quite definite law of development in the nature of the human being which I should like to characterise in the following way.

While the human being is growing into the physical, earthly world, his inner nature is developing in such a way that this development proceeds in the first place out of gesture, out of differentiation of movement. In the inner nature of the organism speech develops out of movement in all its aspects, and thought develops out of speech. This deeply significant law underlies all human development. Everything which makes its appearance in sound, in speech, is the result of gesture, mediated through the inner nature of the human organism.

If you turn your attention to the way in which a child not only learns to speak, but also learns to walk, to place one foot after the other, you can observe how one child treads more strongly on the back part of the foot, on the heel, and another walks more on the toes. You can observe children who in learning to walk tend to bring their legs well forward; with others you will see that they are more inclined to hold back, as it were, between two steps. It is extraordinarily interesting to watch a child learning to walk. You must learn to observe this. But it is more interesting still, although much less attention is

paid to it, to see how a child learns to grasp something, how he
learns to move his hands. There are children who, when they
want something, move their hands in such a way that even the
fingers are brought into movement. Others keep their fingers
still, and stretch out their hands to take hold without moving
the fingers. There are children who stretch out their hand and
arm, while keeping the upper part of the body motionless; there
are others who immediately let the upper part of the body
follow the movement of arm and hand. I once knew a child
who, when he was very small and his high-chair was placed at
a little distance from the table on which stood some dish he
wished to get at, proceeded to "row" himself towards it; his
whole body was then in movement. He could make no movements at all without moving his whole body.

This is the first thing to look out for in a child; for how a
child moves reveals the most inward urge of life, the primal life
impulse. At the same time there appears in the child's movement the tendency to adapt himself to others, to carry out some
movement in the same way as his father, mother or other
member of the family. The principle of imitation comes to light
in gesture, in movement. For gesture is what appears first of all
in human evolution, and in the special constitution of the
physical, soul and spiritual organism of man gesture is inwardly
transformed; it is transformed into speech. Those who are able
to observe this know without any doubt that a child who speaks
as though the sentences were hacked out of him is one who sets
his heels down first; while a child who speaks in such a way
that the sentences run one into the other tends to trip on his
toes. A child who takes hold of things more lightly with his
fingers has the tendency to emphasise the vowel element, while
a child who is inclined to stress the consonants will bring his
whole arm to his aid when grasping something. We receive a
very definite impression of a child's potentialities from his
manner of speaking. And to understand the world, to understand the world through the medium of the senses, through the
medium of thought, this too is developed out of speech.
Thought does not produce speech, but speech thought. So it is

in the cultural development of humanity as a whole; human beings have first spoken, then thought. So it is also with the child; first out of movement he learns to speak, to articulate only then does thinking come forth from speech. We must therefore look upon this sequence as being something of importance : gesture, speech, thought, or the process of thinking.

All this is especially characteristic in the first epoch of the child's life, up to the change of teeth. When little by little the child grows into the world during the first, second, third and fourth years of life, he does so through gesture; everything is dependent on gesture. Indeed, I would say that speaking and thinking take place for the most part unconsciously; both develop naturally out of gesture, even the first gesture. Therefore speaking approximately we can say : From the first to the seventh year gesture predominates in the life of the child, but gesture in the widest sense of the word, gesture which in the child lives in imitation. As educators we must keep this firmly in mind for actually up to the change of teeth the child only takes in what comes to him as gesture, he shuts himself off from everything else. If we say to the child : Do it like this, do it like that, he really does not hear, he does not take any notice. It is only when we stand in front of him and show him how to do it that he is able to copy us. For the child works according to the way I myself am moving my fingers, or he looks at something just as I am looking at it, not according to what I tell him. He imitates everything. This is the secret of the development of the child up to the change of teeth. He lives entirely in imitation, entirely in the imitation of what in the widest possible sense comes to meet him from outside as gesture. This accounts for the surprises we get when faced with the education of very young children. A father came to me once and said, "What shall I do? Something really dreadful has happened. My boy has been stealing." I said, "Let us first find out whether he really steals. What has he done?" The father told me that the boy had taken money out of the cupboard, had bought sweets with it and shared them with the other boys. I said "Presumably that is the cupboard out of which the boy has often seen his mother taking money, before going shopping; he is quite naturally imitating her." And this proved to be the case. So I said further, "But that is not stealing; that lies as a natural principle of development in the boy up to the change of teeth. He imitates what he sees; he must do so." In the presence of a child therefore we should avoid doing anything which he should not imitate. This is how we educate him. If we say : You should not do this or that, it does not influence the child in the slightest degree up to the change of teeth. It could at most have some effect if one were to clothe the words in a gesture, by saying : Now look, you have just done something that I would never do !—for this is in a way a disguised gesture.

It comes to this : with our whole manhood we should fully understand how up to the change of teeth the child is an imitating being. During this time there is actually an inner connection between the child and his environment, between all that is going on around him. Later on this is lost. For however strange and paradoxical it may sound to people today, who are quite unable to think correctly about the spirit, but think always in abstractions, it is nevertheless true that the whole relationship of the child to gesture and movement in his surroundings has an innate religious character. Through his physical body the child is given over to everything in the nature of gesture; he cannot do otherwise than yield himself up to it. What we do later with our soul, and still later with our spirit, in that we yield ourselves up to the divine, even to the external world, as again spiritualised, this the child does with his physical body when he brings it into movement. He is completely immersed in religion, both with his good and his bad qualities. What remains with us as soul and spirit in later life, this the child has also in his physical organism. If therefore the child lives in close proximity with a surly, "bearish" father, liable to fall into rages, someone who is often irritable and angry, expressing uncontrolled emotions in the presence of the child, while the inner causes of such emotions are not as yet understood by the child, nevertheless what he sees, he experiences as something not moral. The child perceives simul-taneously, albeit unconsciously, the moral aspects of these out-breaks, so that he has not only the outer picture of the gesture, but also absorbs its moral significance. If I make an angry gesture, this passes over into the blood organisation of the child, and if these gestures recur frequently they find expression in his blood circulation. The child's physical body is organised according to the way in which I behave in his presence, according to the kind of gestures I make. Moreover if I fail in loving understanding when the child is present, if, without considering him I do something which is only suitable at a later age, and am not constantly on the watch when he is near me, then it can happen that the child enters lovingly into something which is unfitted for his tender years, but belongs to another age, and his physical body will in that case be organised accordingly. Whoever studies the whole course of a man's life from birth to death, bearing in mind the requirements of which I have spoken, will see that a child who has been exposed to things suitable only to grown-up people and who imitates these things will in his later years, from the age of about 50, suffer from sclerosis. One must be able to examine such phenomena in all their ramifications. Illnesses that appear in later life are often only the result of educational errors made in the very earliest years of childhood.

This is why an education which is really based on a knowledge of man must study the human being as a whole from birth until death. To be able to look at man as a whole is the very essence of anthroposophical knowledge. Then too one discovers how very strong the connection is between the child and his environment. I would go as far as to say that the soul of the child goes right out into his surroundings, experiences these surroundings intimately, and indeed has a much stronger relationship to them than at a later period of life. In this respect the child is still very close to the animal, only he experiences things in a more spiritual way, in a way more permeated with soul. The animal's experiences are coarser and cruder, but the animal too is related to its environment. The reason why many phenomena of recent times remain unexplained is because people are not able to enter into all the details involved. There is, for instance, the case of the "calculating horses" which has made such a stir recently, where horses have carried out simple arithmetical operations through stamping with their hooves. I have not seen the famous Elberfelder horses, but I have seen the horse belonging to Herr von Osten. This horse did quite nice little sums. For instance Herr von Osten asked : How much is 5 + 7? And he began to count, beginning with 1, and when he got to 12 the horse stamped with its foot. It could add up, substract and so on. Now there was a young professor who studied this problem and wrote a book about it which is extremely interesting. In this book he expounds the view that the horse sees certain little gestures made by Herr von Osten, who always stands close to the horse. His opinion is that when Herr von Osten counts 7 + 5 up to 12 and the horse stamps when the number 12 is reached, this is because Herr von Osten makes a very slight gesture when he comes to 12 and the horse, noticing this, duly stamps his foot. He believes that it can all be traced back to something visible. But now he puts a question to himself : "Why", he says. "can you not see this gesture which Herr von Osten makes so skilfully that the horse sees it and stamps at the number 12?" The young professor goes on to say that these gestures are so slight that he as a human being cannot see them. From this the conclusion might be drawn that a horse sees more than a professor! But this did not convince me at all, for I saw this wonder of an intelligent horse, the clever Hans, standing by Herr von Osten in his long coat. And I saw too that in his right-hand pocket he had lumps of sugar, and while he was carrying out his experiments with the horse he always handed it one lump after another, so that feeling was aroused in the horse associating sweet things with Herr von Osten. In this way a sort of love was established between Herr von Osten and the horse. And only when this is present, only when the inner being of the horse is, as it were, merged into the inner being of Herr von Osten through the stream of sweetness that flows between them, only then can the horse "calculate", for it really receives something—not through gesture, but through what Herr von Osten is thinking. He thinks: 5 + 7 = 12, and by means of suggestion the horse takes up this thought and even has a distinct impression of it. One can actually see this. The horse and his master are in a certain way merged in feeling one into the other : they impart something to one another reciprocally when they are united through the medium of sweetness. So the animal still has this finer relationship to its environment, and this can be stimulated from outside, as, in this case, by means of sugar.

In a delicate way a similar relationship to the outer world is still present in children also. It lives in the child and should be reckoned with. Education in the kindergarten should therefore never depend on anything other than the principle of imitation. The teacher must sit down with the children and just do what she wishes them to do, so that the child has only to copy. All education and instruction before the change of teeth must be based on this principle.

After the change of teeth all this becomes quite different. The soul life of the child is now completely changed. No longer does he perceive merely the single gestures, but now he sees the way in which these gestures accord with one another. For instance, whereas previously he only had a feeling for a definite line, now he has a feeling for co-ordination, for symmetry. The feeling is awakened for what is co-ordinated or unco-ordinated, and in his soul the child acquires the possibility of perceiving what is formative. As soon as this perception is awakened there appears simultaneously an interest in speech. During the first seven years of life there is an interest in gesture, in everything connected with movement; in the years between seven and fourteen there is an interest in everything connected with the pictorial form, and speech is pre-eminently pictorial and formative. After the change of teeth the child's interest passes over from gesture to speech, and in the lower school years from seven to fourteen we can work most advantageously through everything that lies in speech, above all through the moral element underlying speech. For just as the child before this age has a religious attitude towards the gesture which meets him in the surrounding world, so now he relates himself in a moral sense—his religious feeling being gradually refined into a soul experience—to everything which approaches him through speech.

So now, in this period of his life, one must work upon the child through speech. But whatever is to work upon him in this way must do so by means of an unquestioned authority. When I want to convey to the child some picture expressed through speech, I must do so with the assurance of authority. I must be the unquestioned authority for the child when through speech I want to conjure up before him some picture. Just as we must actually show the little child what we want him to do, so we must be the human pattern for the child between the change of teeth and puberty. In other words, there is no point whatever in giving reasons to a child of this age, in trying to make him see why we should do something or not do it, just because there are well-founded reasons for or against it. This passes over the child's head. It is important to understand this. In exactly the same way as in the earliest years of life the child only observes the gesture, so between the change of teeth and puberty he only observes what I, as a human being, am in relation to himself. At this age the child must, for instance, learn about what is moral in such a way that he regards as good what the naturally accepted authority of the teacher, by means of speech, designates as good; he must regard as bad what this authority designates as bad. The child must learn : What my teacher, as my authority, does is good, what he does not do is bad. Relatively speaking then, the child feels : When my teacher says something is good, then it is good; and if he says something is bad, then it is bad. You will not attribute to me, seeing that 30 years ago I wrote my *Philosophy of Freedom*,* a point of view which upholds the principle of authority as the one and only means of salvation. But through the very fact of knowing the true nature of freedom one also knows that between the change of teeth and puberty the child needs to be faced with an unquestioned authority. This lies in the nature of man. Everything is

---

* Also called *The Philosophy of Spiritual Activity* in some English translations.

doomed to failure in education which disregards this relationship of the child to the unquestioned authority of the personality of the teacher and educator. The child must be guided in
everything which he should do or not do, think or not think,
feel or not feel, by what flows to him, by way of speech, from
his teacher and educator. At this age therefore there is no
sense in wanting to approach him through the intellect. During this time everything must be directed towards the life of
feeling, for feeling is receptive to anything in the nature of
pictures and the child of this age is so constituted that he lives
in the world of pictures, of images, and has the feeling of
welding separate details into a harmonious whole. This is why,
for instance, what is moral cannot be brought to the child by
way of precept, by saying : You should do this, you should
not do that. It simply doesn't work. What does work is when
the child, through the way in which one speaks to him, can
feel inwardly in his soul a liking for what is good, a dislike of
what is bad. Between the change of teeth and puberty the
child is an aesthete and we must therefore take care that he
experiences pleasure in the good and displeasure in what is
bad. This is the best way for him to develop a sense of
morality.

We must also be sincere, inwardly sincere in the imagery we
use in our work with the child. This entails being permeated to
the depths of our being by everything we do. This is not the
case if, when standing before the child we immediately experience a slight sense of superiority : I am so clever—the child is
so stupid. Such an attitude ruins all education; it also destroys
in the child the feeling for authority. Well then, how shall I
transform into a pictorial image something that I want to
impart to the child? In order to make this clear I have chosen
the following example as an illustration.

We cannot speak to the child about the immortality of the
soul in the same way as to a grown-up person; but we must
nevertheless convey to him some understanding of it. We must
however do so in a pictorial way. We must build up the
following picture and to do this may well take the whole lesson.

We can explain to the child what a butterfly's chrysalis is, and then speak in some such words as these: "Well, later on the finished butterfly flies out of the chrysalis. It was inside all the time only it was not yet visible, it was not yet ready to fly away, but it was already there inside." Now we can go further and tell him that in a similar way the human body contains the soul, only it is not visible. At death the soul flies out of the body; the only difference between man and butterfly is that the butterfly is visible and the human soul is invisible. In this way we can speak to the child about the immortality of the soul so that he receives a true picture of immortality and one suited to his age. But in the presence of the child we must on no account have the feeling: I am clever, I am a philosopher and by no means of thought can I convince myself of the truth of immortality; the child is naïve, is stupid, and so for him I will build up the picture of the butterfly creeping out of the chrysalis. If one thinks in this way one establishes no contact with the child, and then he gets nothing whatever from what he is told. There is only one possibility. We must ourselves believe in the picture, we must not want to be cleverer than the child; we must stand in the presence of the child as full of belief as he is. How can this be done? An anthroposophist, a student of spiritual science knows that the emergence of the butterfly from the chrysalis *is* actually a picture of the immortality of the human soul placed into the world by the gods. He can never think otherwise than that the gods inscribed into the world this picture of the emerging butterfly as an image of the immortality of the human soul. In all the lower stages of the process he sees the higher processes which have become abstract. If I do not get the idea that the child is stupid and I am clever, but if I stand before the child conscious that this actually is so in the world and that I am leading him to believe in something which I too believe with all my heart, then there arises an imponderable relationship between us, and the child makes real progress in his education. Then moral imponderabilia continually enters into our educational relationship. And this is the crux of the matter.

When we are quite clear about this we shall, out of the whole nexus of our studies, come to see how we can find the right approach to an instruction which is truly educational, an education which really instructs. Let us take an example. How must the child learn to read and write? There is actually a great deal more misery connected with this than one usually imagines, though human intellectualism is far too crude to perceive it. One recognises that learning to read and write is a necessity, so it follows that the child must at all costs be drilled into learning reading and writing. But just consider what this means for a child! When they are grown-up, people have no inclination to put themselves in the child's place, to imagine what he undergoes when he learns to read and write. In our civilisation today we have letters, a, b, c and so on; they are there before us in certain definite forms. Now the child has the sound a (ah, as in *father*). When does he use it? This sound is for him the expression of an inner soul experience. He uses this sound when he is faced with something which calls up in him a feeling of wonder, of astonishment. This sound he understands. It is bound up with human nature. Or he has the sound e (eh, as in *they*). When does he use this? He uses it when he wants to show he has the feeling: "Something has come up against me; I have experienced something which encroaches on my own nature." If somebody gives me a blow, I say e (eh).* It is the same with the consonants. Every sound corresponds to some expression of life; the consonants imitate an outer, external world, the vowels express what is experienced inwardly in the soul. The study of language, philology, is today only approaching the first elements of such things.

Learned scholars, who devote themselves to research into language, have given much thought to what, in the course of human evolution, may have been the origin of speech. There are two theories. The one represents the view that speech may have arisen out of soul experiences in much the same way as

* In English we tend to prefix an aspirate to the vowel, saying "Ha" when something astonishes us, or "Heh" when something impinges on us, e.g. "Heh, stop it!"

this takes place in the animal, albeit in its most primitive form—"moo-moo" being the expression of what the cow feels inwardly, and "bow-wow" what is experienced by the dog. And so, in a more complicated way, what in man becomes articulated speech arises out of this urge to give expression to inner feelings and experiences. In somewhat humorous vein this is called the "bow-wow theory". The other point of view proceeds from the supposition that in the sounds of speech man imitates what takes place in the outer world. It is possible to imitate the sound of a bell, what is taking place inside the bell: "ding-dong—ding-dong". Here there is the attempt to imitate what takes place in the outer world. This is the basis for the theory that in speech everything may be traced back to external sounds, external event. It is the "ding-dong theory". So we have these two theories in opposition to one another. It is not in any way my intention to make fun of this, for as a matter of fact, both are correct : the "bow-wow" theory is right for the vowel element in speech, the "ding-dong" theory for the consonantal element. In transposing gestures into sounds we learn by means of the consonants to imitate inwardly outer processes; and in the vowels we give form to inner experiences of the soul. In speech the inner and the outer unite. Human nature, itself homogeneous, understands how to bring this about.

We receive the child into the primary school. Through his inner organisation he has become a being able to speak. Now, suddenly he is expected to experience—I say experience deliberately weighing my words, not recognise, *experience*—a connection between astonishment, wonder, (ah) and the demonic sign *a*. This is something completely foreign to him. He is supposed to learn something which he feels to be utterly remote, and to relate this to the sound "ah". This is something outside the sphere of a young child's comprehension. He feels it as a veritable torture if at the very outset we confront him with the forms of the letters in use today.

We can, however, remember something else. The letters which we have today were not always there. Let us look back to those ancient peoples who had a picture writing. They used pictures to give tangible form to what was uttered, and these pictures certainly had something to do with what they were intended to express. They did not have letters such as we use, but pictures which were related to their meaning. Up to a certain point the same could be said of cuneiform writing. These were times when people still had a human relationship to things, even when these were fixed into a definite form. Today we no longer have this, but with the child we must go back to it again. We must of course not do so in such a way that we study the cultural history of ancient peoples and fall back on the forms which were once used in picture writing; but we must bring all our educational fantasy into play as teachers in order to create the kind of pictures we need. Fantasy, imagination* we must certainly have, for without it we cannot be teachers or educators. And so it is always necessary to refer to the importance of enthusiasm, of inspiration, when dealing with some characteristic feature of anthroposophy. It never gives me any pleasure, for instance, when I go into a class in our Waldorf School and notice that a teacher is tired and is teaching out of a certain mood of weariness. That is something one must never do. One simply cannot be tired, one can only be filled with enthusiasm. When teaching, one must be absolutely on the spot with one's whole being. It is quite wrong to be tired when teaching; tiredness must be kept for some other occasion. The essential thing for a teacher is that he learns to give full play to his fantasy. What does this mean? To begin with I call up in the child's mind something that he has seen at the market, or some other place, a fish for example. I next get him to draw a fish, and for this I even allow him to use colours, so that he paints as he draws and draws as he paints. This being achieved I then let him say the word "Fish", not speaking the word quickly, but separating the sounds, "f-i-ssh". Then I lead him on so that he says only the beginning of the word fish (f . . .) and gradually I transfer the shape of the fish into a

* The German *phantasie* is often more equivalent to the English *imagination* than to *fantasy*. In this lecture the latter is probably more appropriate.

sign that is somewhat fish like, while at the same time getting
the child to say f . . . And there we have it, the letter "f"!

Or I let the child say Wave (W-a-v-e) showing him at the same
time what a wave is (see sketch). Once again I let him paint
this and get him to say the beginning of the word—w—and
then I change the picture of a wave into the letter w.

Continuing to work in the same way I allow the written
characters gradually to emerge from the painting-drawing and
drawing-painting, as indeed they actually arose in the first
place. I do not bring the child into a stage of civilisation with
which as yet he has nothing in common, but I guide him in
such a way that he is never torn away from his relationship to
the outer world. In order to do this there is no necessity to
study the history of culture—albeit the writing in use today has
arisen out of picture-writing—one must only give free play
to one's fantasy, for then one brings the child to the point at
which he is able to form writing out of this drawing and
painting.

Now we must not think of this only as an ingenious and
clever new method. We must value the fact that the child
unites himself inwardly with something that is new to him when

his soul activity is constantly stimulated. He does not "grow into it" when he is pushed, so that he is always coming into an unfamiliar relationship with his environment. The whole point is that we are working on the inner being of the child.

What is usually done today? It is perhaps already somewhat out-of-date, but not so long ago people gave little girls "beautiful" dolls, with real hair, dolls that could shut their eyes when one laid them down, dolls with pretty faces and so on. Civilisation calls them beautiful, but they are nevertheless hideous, because they are inartistic. What sort of dolls are these? They are the sort which cannot activate the child's fantasy. Now let us do something different. Tie a handkerchief so that you have a figure with arms and legs; then make eyes with blobs of ink and perhaps a mouth with red ink as well; now the child must develop his fantasy if he is to imagine this as having the human shape. Such a thing works with tremendous living force on the child, because it offers him the possibility of using his fantasy. Naturally one must do this first oneself. But the possibility must be provided for the child, and this must be done at the age when everything is play. It is for this reason that all those things which do not stimulate fantasy in the child are so damaging when given as toys. As I said, today these beautiful dolls are somewhat out-dated, for now we give children monkeys or bears. To be sure, neither do these toys give any opportunity for the unfolding of a fantasy having any relationship to the human being. Let us suppose that a child runs up to us and we give him a bear to cuddle. Things like this show clearly how far our civilisation is from being able to penetrate into the depths of human nature. But it is quite remarkable how children in a perfectly natural, artistic way are able to form imaginatively a picture of this inner side of human nature.

In the Waldorf School we have made a transition from the ordinary methods of teaching to what may be termed a teaching through art, and this quite apart from the fact that in no circumstances do we begin by teaching the children to write, but we let them paint as they draw, and draw as they paint. Perhaps we might even say that we let them splash about, which involves the possibly tiresome job of cleaning up the classroom afterwards. I shall also speak tomorrow about how to lead over from writing to reading, but, quite apart from this painting and drawing, we guide the child as far as possible into the realm of the artistic by letting him practise modelling in his own little way, but without suggesting that he should make anything beyond what he himself wants to fashion out of his own inner being. The results are quite remarkable. I will mention one example which shows how something very wonderful takes place in the case of rather older children.

At a comparatively early age, that is to say, for children between ten and eleven years old, we take as a subject in our curriculum the "Study of Man". At this age the children learn to know how the bones are formed and built up, how they support each other, and so on. They learn this in an artistic way, not intellectually. After a few such lessons the child has acquired some perception of the structure of the human bones, the dynamic of the bones and their interdependence. Then we go over to the craft-room, where the children model plastic forms and we observe what they are making. We see that they have learned something from these lessons about the bones. Not that the child imitates the forms of the bones, but from the way in which he now models his forms we perceive the outer expression of an inner mobility of soul. Before this he has already got so far as to be able to make little receptacles of various kinds; children discover how to make bowls and similar things quite by themselves, but what they make out of the spontaneity of childhood before they have received such lessons is quite different from what they model afterwards, provided they have really experienced what was intended. In order to achieve this result, however, these lessons on the "Knowledge of Man" must be given in such a way that their content enters right into the whole human being. Today this is difficult.

Anyone who has paid as many visits to studios as I have and seen how people paint and model and carve, knows very well that today hardly any sculptor works without a model; he must have a human form in front of him if he wishes to model it.

This would have had no sense for a Greek artist. He had of course learned to know the human form in the public games, but he really experienced it inwardly. He knew out of his own inner feeling—and this feeling he embodied without the aid of a model—he knew the difference between an arm when it is stretched out or when, in addition, the forefinger is also extended, and this feeling he embodied in his sculpture. Today, however, when physiology is taught in the usual way, models or drawings of the bones are placed side by side, the muscles are described one after another and no impression is given of their reciprocal relationship. With us, when the children see a vertebra belonging to the spinal column, they know how similar it is to the skull-bone, and they get a feeling for the metamorphosis of the bones. In this way they enter livingly right into the different human forms and so feel the urge to express it artistically. Such an experience enters right into life; it does not remain external.

My earnest wish, and also my duty as leader of the Waldorf School, is to make sure that wherever possible everything of a fixed nature in the way of science, everything set down in books in a rigid scientific form should be excluded from class teaching. Not that I do not value science; no one could value science more highly. Such studies can be indulged in outside the school, if so desired; but I should be really furious if I were to see a teacher standing in front of a class with a book in his or her hand. In teaching everything must come from within. This must be self-understood. How is botany taught today for instance? We have botany books; these are based on a scientific outlook, but they do not belong to the classroom where there are children between the change of teeth and puberty. The perception of what a teacher needs in the way of literature must be allowed to grow gradually out of the living educational principles I shall be speaking about here.

So we are really concerned with the teacher's attitude of mind, whether in soul, spirit and body he is able to relate himself to the world. If he has this living relationship he can do much with the children between the change of teeth and puberty, for he is then their natural and accepted authority. The main thing is that one should enter into and experience things in a living way and carry over into life all that one has thus experienced. This is the great and fundamental principle which must form the basis of education today. Then the connection with the class will be there of itself, together with the imponderable mood and feeling that must necessarily go with it.

ANSWER TO A QUESTION

Question : There are grown-up people who seem to have remained at the imitative stage of childhood. Why is this?

Dr. Steiner : It is possible at every stage of human development for someone to remain in a stationary condition. If we describe the different stages of development, adding to today's survey the embryonic stage, and continuing to the change of teeth, and on to puberty, we cover those epochs in which a fully developed human life can be formed. Now quite a short time ago the general trend of anthroposophical development brought it about that lectures could be held on curative education, with special reference to definite cases of children who had either remained backward or whose development was in some respect abnormal. We then took the further step of allowing certain cases to be seen which were being treated at Dr. Wegmann's Clinical-Therapeutic Institute. Among these cases there was one of a child of nearly a year old, about the normal size for a child of this age, but who in the formation of his physical body had remained approximately at the stage of seven or eight months embryo. If you were to draw the child in outline with only an indication of the limbs, which are somewhat more developed, but showing exactly the form of the head, as it actually is in the case of this little boy, then, looking cursorily at the drawing, you would not have the faintest idea that it is a boy of nearly a year old. You would think it an embryo, because this boy has in many respects kept after his birth the embryonic structure.

Every stage of life, including the embryonic, can be carried over into a later stage; for the different phases of development as they follow one after the other, are such that each new phase is a metamorphosis of the old, with something new added. If you will only take quite exactly what I have already said in regard to the natural religious devotion of the child to his surroundings up to the change of teeth, you will see that this changes later into the life of soul, and you have, as a second attribute the aesthetic, artistic stage. Now it happens with very many children that the first stage is carried into the second, and the latter then remains poorly developed. But this can go still further: the first stage of physical embodiment can be carried over into each of the others, so that what was present as the original stage appears in all the later stages. And, for a superficial observation of life, it need not be so very obvious that an earlier stage has remained on into a later one, unless such a condition shows itself particularly late in life. Certain it is however that earlier stages are carried over into later ones.

Let us take the same thing in a lower kingdom of nature. The fully grown, fully developed plant usually has root, stalk, with it cotyledon leaves, followed by the later green leaves. These are then concentrated in the calyx, the petals, the stamen, the pistil and so on. There are however plants which do not develop as far as the blossom, but remain behind at the stage of herbs and other plants where the green leaves remain stationary, and the fruit is merely rudimentary. How far, for instance, the fern has remained behind the buttercup! With the plant this does not lead to abnormality. Man however is a species for himself. He is a complete natural order. And it can happen that someone remains his whole life long an imitative being, or one who stands in need of authority. For in life we have not only to do with people who remain at the imitative stage, but also with those who in regard to their essential characteristics remain at the stage that is fully developed between the change of teeth and puberty. As a matter of fact there are very many such people, and with them this stage continues into later life. They cannot progress much farther, and what should be developed in later years can only do so to a limited extent. They remain always at the stage where they look for the support of authority. If there were no such people, neither would there be the tendency, so rife today, to form sects and such things, for sectarian associations are based on the fact that their adherents are not required to think; they leave the thinking to others and follow their leaders. In certain spheres of life, however, most people remain at the stage of authority. For instance, when it is a question of forming a judgment about something of a scientific nature people do not take the trouble to look into it themselves, but they ask : Where is the expert who must know about this, the specialist who is a lecturer at one of the universities? There you have the principle of authority. Again in the case of people who are ill the principle of authority is carried to extremes, even though here it may be justifiable. And in legal matters, for instance, nobody today will think of forming an independent judgment, but will seek the advice of a solicitor because he has the requisite knowledge. Here the standpoint is that of an eight or nine year old child. And it may well be that this solicitor himself is not much older. When a question is put to him he takes down a lawbook or portfolio and there again you have an authority. So it is actually the case that each stage of life can enter into a later one.

The Anthroposophical Society should really only consist of people who are outgrowing authority, who do not recognise any such principle but only true insight. This is so little understood by people outside the Society that they are continually saying: "Anthroposophy is based on authority." In reality the precise opposite is the case; the principle of authority must be outgrown through the kind of understanding and discernment which is fostered in anthroposophy. The important thing is that one should grasp every scrap of insight one can lay hold of in order to pass through the different stages of life.

LECTURE IV

Arnheim, 20th July, 1924

Arising out of yesterday's lecture a further question has been put to me in connection with our subject and I should like to deal with it here. The question is this : "With reference to the law of imitation in a child's movements I regard as important an explanation of the following fact. My grandfather died when my father was between eighteen months and two years old. When he was about forty-five my father visited one of my grandfather's friends who was astonished at the similarity of all my father's movements and gestures with those of my grandfather. What was the cause of this, seeing that owing to my grandfather's early death there could hardly be any question of imitation !

So a man died when his son was between eighteen months and two years old and long afterwards, when the latter was in his 45th year, he heard from this friend, who was in a position to know, that as late as his 45th year he still imitated, or rather had the same gestures as his father.

Of course we are dealing here with matters of such a nature that it is scarcely possible to do more than give certain guiding lines, omitting detailed explanations. Unfortunately our courses of lectures are short, and the theme, if it were to be gone into fully, would need many lectures and ample time, six months for instance, or even a whole year. Very many questions are therefore likely to arise, and it may well be possible to answer these if they are brought forward. I must however point out that owing to the limited time at our disposal a certain lack of clarity will inevitably arise and this could only be cleared up if it were possible to enter fully into every detail. With reference to the question which has been put I should like to interpolate the following remarks.

If we take the first epoch of a child's life, that is, the time between birth and the change of teeth, the organisation of the child is working and developing in such a way that those predispositions are incorporated into the organism which I described yesterday as consisting of walking, which includes the general orientation of the human being, of speaking and thirdly of thinking.

Now this is how things follow one another. Between the first and seventh year of life the child is so organised that he is mainly concerned with gesture; between approximately the seventh and fourteenth year he is concerned with speech, as I explained yesterday; and, again speaking approximately, between his fourteenth and twenty-first year he is so organised that he is mainly concerned with thinking. What thus makes its appearance in the course of twenty-one years is however already taking shape as predisposition in the first period of life, between birth and the change of teeth. In so far as the assimilation of gesture is concerned, and this includes walking freely in space without need of support, so that the arms and also the muscles of the face can move in an expressive way—in other words a general orientation, finding a living relationship with gesture and movement—all this is developed mainly in the first third of these years, that is to say in the first $2\frac{1}{3}$ years. The main development of the child during this time lies in the unfolding and building up of gesture. The gestures then continue to develop, but in addition something more intimate and inward is now impressed into the speech organism. Although the child has already uttered a few words nevertheless the experience of speech as predisposition takes place after $2\frac{1}{3}$ years. The actual experience and feeling for speech is fully developed between the seventh and fourteenth year, but as predisposition it is there between $2\frac{1}{3}$ and $4\frac{2}{3}$ years old. Naturally all this must be taken as an average. From then on the child develops the faculty of experiencing inwardly the first beginnings of thought. What unfolds and blossoms later, between the 14th and 21st year is already developing germinally between $4\frac{2}{3}$ and 7 years old. The forming of gestures continues of course throughout these years, but other faculties enter in. We see therefore that in the main we have to place the time for the unfolding and forming of gestures right back to the first $2\frac{1}{2}$ years. What is gained during this time lies deepest. This is only natural, for we can well imagine how fundamentally the principle of imitation works in the very first years of life.

If you take all this together you will no longer find anything astonishing in what gave rise to the question that has been put here. The grandfather died when the father was between $1\frac{1}{2}$ and 2 years old. Now this is precisely the time in which the forming of gesture is working most deeply. If the grandfather died then, the gestures the child imitated from him made by far the deepest impression. That is in no way altered by what may have been imitated later from other people. So just this particular case is extraordinarily significant when we consider it in detail.

We tried yesterday to explain how in the second period of life, between the change of teeth and puberty, the child in the course of his development experiences everything that finds its expression through speech, in which the self-understood authority of the teacher and educator must play its part. The intercourse between teacher and child must be of such a kind that it works in a pictorial, imaginative way. And I pointed out how at this age one cannot approach the child with moral precepts but can only work effectively on his moral nature by awakening in him such feelings as can be awakened by pictures: so that the child receives pictures described by his teacher and educator, who is also his model. These work in such a way that what is good pleases him and what is bad gives him a feeling of distaste. Therefore at this preparatory or elementary school age morality must be instilled in pictorial form by way of the feelings.

I explained further how writing must be brought to the child in a pictorial way and I showed how the forms of the letters must be developed out of the drawing-painting and the painting-drawing. Of all the arts this must be cultivated first, for it leads the child into civilisation. Everything which introduces the child at the very outset into the forms of the letters, which are completely strange to him, is quite wrong from an educational point of view; for the finished forms of the letters used in our present day civilisation work on the child like little demons.

Now in an education built up on a knowledge of man, learning to write must precede learning to read. If you want to come near to a child of this age, immediately after the change of teeth, you must as far as possible approach the whole being of the child. The child when occupied in writing does at least bring the whole of the upper part of the body into activity; there is an inner mobility which is quite different from when only the head is kept busy learning the forms of the letters. The emancipated, independent faculties of the head can only be made use of at a later age. For this reason we can make a transition by allowing the child also to read what he has written. In this way an impression is made on him.

By carrying out our teaching in this way at the Waldorf School it transpired that our children learn to read somewhat later than others; they even learn to write the letters a little later than children in other schools. It is necessary however, before forming a judgment in regard to this to be able really to enter into the nature of man with understanding. With the limited perception and feeling for a knowledge of man usual at the present day, people do not notice at all how detrimental it is for the general development of the human being if, as a child, he learns too early things so remote from him as reading and writing. Certainly nobody will experience any deficiency in his capacity to read and write, whose proficiency in these arts is attained somewhat later than others; on the other hand everyone who learns to read and write too early will suffer in this very respect. An education based on a knowledge of man must from the very beginning, proceed out of this ability to read human evolution and by understanding the conditions of life help the child in furthering the development of his own nature. This is the one and only way to a really health-giving education.

To gain deeper insight we must enter somewhat into the being of man. In man we have in the first place his physical body which is most intensively developed in the first epoch of life. In the second epoch the higher, finer body, the etheric body, develops predominantly. Now it is a matter of great importance that in this study of man we should proceed in a truly scientific way, and we must conjure up the same courage as is shown today in other branches of science. A substance showing a definite degree of warmth, can be brought into a condition in which that warmth, hitherto bound up with substance, becomes freed. It is liberated and then becomes "free" warmth. In the case of mineral substances we have the courage to speak scientifically when we say that there is "bound" warmth and "free" warmth. We must acquire the same courage when we study the world as a whole. If we have this courage then the following reveals itself to us in regard to man.

We can ask : Where are the forces of the etheric body in the first epoch of life? During this time they are bound up with the physical body and are active in its nourishment and growth. In this first epoch the child is different from what he becomes later. The entire forces of the etheric body are at first bound up with the physical body. At the end of the first epoch they are freed to some extent, just as warmth becomes free from the substances with which it was formerly bound up. What takes place now? Only a part of the etheric body is working after the change of teeth in the forces of growth and nourishment; the freed part becomes the bearer of the more intensive development of the memory, of qualities of soul. We must learn to speak of a soul that is "bound" during the first seven years of life and of a soul that has become free after the 7th year. For it is so. What we use as forces of the soul in the second seven years of life is imperceptibly bound up with the physical body during the first seven years; this is why nothing of a psychic nature becomes body free. A knowledge of how the soul works in the first seven years of life must be gained from observation of the body. And only after the change of teeth can any direct approach be made to what is purely of a soul nature.

This is a way of looking at things which leads directly from the physical to the psychological. Just think of the many different approaches to psychology today. They are based on speculation pure and simple. People think things over and discover that on the one hand we have the soul and on the other hand the body. Now the following question arises: Does the body work on the soul as its original cause, or is it the other way round? If they get no further either way, they discover something so extraordinarily grotesque as psychophysical parallelism, the idea of which is that both manifestations run parallel, side by side. In this way no explanation is given for the interaction of one with the other, but one speaks only of parallelism. This is a sign that nothing is known about these things out of experience. Out of experience one would have to say: In the first seven years of a child's life one perceives the soul working in the body. How it works must be learned through observation, not through mere speculation. Anthroposophy as a means of knowledge rejects all speculation and proceeds everywhere from experience, but of course from physical and spiritual experience.

So in the second period of life, in the time between the change of teeth and puberty the etheric body of man is our chief concern in education. Both teacher and child need above all those forces which are working in the etheric body, for these release the feeling life of the child, not yet judgment and thought. Deeply embedded in the nature of the child between the change of teeth and puberty is the third member of the human being, the astral body, which is the bearer of all feeling life and sensation. During this second period of life the astral body is still deeply embedded in the etheric body. Therefore, because the etheric body is now relatively free, we have the task to develop it in such a way that it can follow its own tendencies, helped and not hindered by education. When can it be so helped? This can happen when in the widest possible sense we teach and educate the child by means of pictures, when we build up imaginatively and pictorially everything that we wish him to absorb. For the etheric body is the body of formative forces; it models the wonderful forms of the organs, heart, lungs, liver and so on. The physical body which we inherit acts only as a model; after the first seven years, after the change of teeth, it is laid aside, and the second physical body is fashioned by the etheric body. This is why at this age we must educate in a way that is adapted to the plastic formative forces of the etheric body.

Now, just as we teach the child by means of pictures, just as, among other things, he learns to write by a kind of painting-drawing—and we cannot introduce the child too early to what is artistic, for our entire teaching must be permeated with artistic feeling—so must we also bear the following in mind. Just as the etheric body is inseparably associated with what is formative and pictorial, so the astral body, which underlies the life of feeling and sensation, tends in its organisation towards the musical nature of man. To what then must we look when we observe the child? Because the astral body between the change of teeth and puberty is still embedded in the physical and etheric bodies every child whose soul life is healthy is inwardly deeply musical. Every healthy child is inwardly deeply musical. We have only to call up this musicality by making use of the child's natural liveliness and sense of movement. Artistic teaching therefore must, from the very beginning of school life, make use both of the plastic and pictorial arts and also of the art of music. Nothing abstract must be allowed to dominate; it is the artistic approach which is all-important, and out of what is artistic the child must be led to a comprehension of the world.

But now we must proceed in such a way that the child learns gradually to find his own orientation in the world. I have already said that it is most repugnant to me if I see scientific text books brought into school and the teaching carried out along those lines. For today in our scientific work, which I fully recognise, we have deviated in many respects from a conception of the world which is in accordance with nature. We will now ask ourselves the following question, bearing in mind that in the course of discussion other things may have to be added. At about what age can one begin to teach children about the plant world?

This must be done neither too late nor too early. We must be aware that a very important stage in a child's development is reached between the 9th and 10th year. Those who see with the eye of a teacher observe this in every child. There comes a time in which the child, although he does not usually express it in words, nevertheless shows in his whole behaviour that he has a question, or a number of questions, which betray an inner crisis in his life. This is an exceptionally delicate experience in the child and an exceptionally delicate sense for these things is necessary if one is to perceive it. But it is there and it must be observed. At this age the child learns quite instinctively to differentiate himself from the outer world. Up to this time the "I" and the outer world interpenetrate each other, and it is therefore possible to tell the child stories about animals, plants and stones in which they all behave as though they were human beings. Indeed this is the best approach, for we should appeal to the child's pictorial, imaginative sense, and this we do if we speak about the kingdoms of nature in this way. Between the 9th and 10th year however the child learns to say "I" in full consciousness. He learns this earlier of course, but now he does so consciously. These years, therefore, when the consciousness of the child is no longer merged with the outer world, but when he learns to differentiate himself from it, are the time when we can begin, without immediately renouncing the pictorial element, to lead the child to an understanding of the plant world, but to an understanding imbued with feeling.

Today we are accustomed to look at one plant alongside of another, we know their names and so on; we do this as though the single plant was there for itself. But when we study the plant in this way, it is just as if you were to pull out a hair, and forgetting that it was on your head examine it for itself, in the belief that you can know something about its nature and life-conditions without considering it as growing out of your head. The hair only has meaning when it is growing on the head; it cannot be studied for itself. It is the same with the plant. One cannot pull it up and study it separately, but one must consider the whole earth as an organism to which the plants belong. This is actually what it is. The plants belong to the entire growth of the earth, in the same way as the hairs belong to our head. Plants can never be studied in an isolated way, but only in connection with the whole nature of the earth. The earth and the world of plants belong together.

Let us suppose that you have a herbaceous plant, an annual, which is growing out of the root, shooting up into stalk, leaves and flowers, and developing the fruit which is sown again in the following year. Then you have the earth underneath, in which the plant is growing. But now, think of a tree. The tree lives longer, it is not an annual. It develops around itself the mineralised bark which is of such a nature that pieces of it can be broken off. What is this in reality? The process is as follows : If you were to pile up around a plant the surrounding earth with its inherent forces, if you were more or less to cover it with earth, then you would bring this about in an external, mechanical way, through human activity. Nature however does the same thing by wrapping the tree round with the bark; only in this case it is not completely earth. In the bark there is a kind of hill of earth, the earth heaps itself up. We can see the earth flourishing and growing when we see the growing tree. This is why what surrounds the root of the plant must most certainly be reckoned as belonging to it. We must regard the soil as belonging to the plant.

Anyone who has trained himself to observe such things and happens to travel in a district where he notices many plants with yellow flowers will at once look to see what kind of soil it is. In such a case, where specifically many yellow flowers are to be seen, one is likely to find, for instance, a soil which is somewhat red in colour. You will never be able to think about the plant without taking into consideration the earth in which it grows. Both belong together. And one should lose no time in accustoming oneself to this; as otherwise one destroys in oneself a sense for realities.

A deep impression was made on me recently, when at the request of certain farmers, I gave an agricultural course, at the end of which a farmer said : Today everybody knows that our vegetables are dying out, are becoming decadent and this with alarming rapidity. Why is this? It is because people no longer understand, as they understood in bygone days, as the peasants understood, that earth and plants are bound together and must be so considered. If we want to foster the well-being of our vegetables so that they flourish again we must understand how to treat them in the right way, in other words, we must give them the right kind of manure. We must give the earth the possibility of living rightly in the environment of the plant roots. Today, after the failure of agricultural methods of development, we need a new impulse in agriculture based on Spiritual Science. This will enable us to make use of manure in such a way that the growth of plants does not degenerate. Anyone as old as I am can say : I know how potatoes looked 50 years ago in Europe—and how they look today! Today we have not only the decline of the West in regard to its cultural life, but this decline penetrates deeply also into the kingdoms of nature, for example, in regard to agriculture.

It really amounts to this, that the sense for the connection between the plant and its environment should not be destroyed, that on school outings and similar occasions the plants should not be uprooted and put into specimen containers and then brought into the classroom in the belief that thereby something has been achieved. For the uprooted plant can never exist just for itself. Today people indulge in totally unreal ideas. For instance they look upon a piece of chalk and a flower as having reality in the same sense. But what nonsense this is! The mineral can exist for itself, it can really do this. So the plant also (they say) should have an independent existence;

but it cannot, it ceases to be when it is uprooted from the ground. It only has earthly existence when it is attached to something other than itself, and that other only has existence in so far as it is part of the whole earth. We must study things as they are in their totality, not tear them out of it.

Almost all our knowledge based on observation teems with unrealities of this kind. This is why Nature Study has become completely abstract, although this is partly justified, as with the theory of relativity. Anyone, however, who can think in a realistic way cannot allow abstract concepts to run on and on, but notices when they cease to have any relationship with what is real. This is something he finds painful. Naturally you can follow the laws of acoustics and say : When I make a sound, the transmission of this sound has a definite speed. When I hear a sound anywhere, at any particular place, I can calculate the exact time its transmission will take. If now I move, no matter at what speed, in the direction the sound is travelling, I shall hear it later. Should my speed exceed the speed of the sound I shall not hear it at all; but if I move towards the sound I shall hear it earlier. The theory of relativity has its definite justification. According to this, however, we can also come to the following conclusion : If I now move towards the sound more quickly than the sound travels, I shall finally go beyond it, so that I shall hear the sound before it is made! This is obvious to anyone able to think realistically. Such a person also knows that logically it is absolutely correct, wonderfully thought out, to say that a clock (to take the famous comparison of Einstein) thrown with the speed of light into universal space and returning from thence, will not have changed in any respect. This can be wonderfully thought out. But for a realistic thinker the question must necessarily arise : What will the clock look like on its return? for he does not separate his thinking from reality, he remains always in the sphere of reality.

This is the essential characteristic of Spiritual Science. It never demands a merely logical approach, but one in accordance with reality. That is why people today, who carry abstractions even to the splitting of hairs, reproach us anthroposophists with being abstract, just because our way of thinking seeks everywhere the absolute reality, never losing the connection with reality, although here certainly the spiritual reality has to be included and understood. This is why it is possible to perceive so clearly how unnatural it is to connect plant study with specimens in a container.

It is therefore important when introducing the child to plant study that we consider the actual face of the earth and deal with the soil and plant growth as a whole, so that the child will never think of the plant as something detached and separate. This can be unpleasant for the teacher, for now he cannot take the usual botany books into class with him, have a quick glance at them during the lesson and behave as though he knew it all perfectly. I have already said that today there are no suitable botany text-books. But this sort of teaching takes on another aspect when one knows the effect of the imponderable and when one considers that in the child the subconscious works still more strongly than in older people. This subconscious is terribly clever and anyone able to perceive the spiritual life of the child knows that when a class is seated facing the teacher and he walks up and down with his notes and wants to impart the content of these notes to the children, they always form a judgment and think; Well, why should I know that? He doesn't even know it himself! This disturbs the lesson tremendously, for these feelings rise up out of the subconscious and nothing can be expected of a class which is taught by someone with notes in his hand.

We must always look into the spiritual side of things. This is particularly necessary when developing the art of education, for by doing so we can create in the child a feeling of standing firmly and safely in the world. For (in lessons on the plant) he gradually grasps the idea that the earth is an organism. And this it actually is and when it begins to become lifeless we must help it by making the right use of manure. For instance, it is not true that the water contained in the air is the same as that in the earth below. The water below has a certain vitality; the water above loses this vitality and only regains it when it descends. All these things are real, absolutely real. If we do not grasp them we do not unite ourselves with the world in a real way. This then is what I wished to say in regard to the teaching about the world of plants.

Now we come to the animal world and we cannot consider the animals as belonging to the earth in the same way. This is apparent from the mere fact that the animals can move about; in this respect they are independent. But when we compare the animals with man we find something very characteristic in their formation. This has always been indicated in an older, instinctive science, the after-effects of which still remained in the first third of the 19th century. When however a modern man with his way of looking at things reads the opinions expressed by those philosophers of nature who, following old traditions, still regarded the animal world in its relation to the human world, these strike him as being utterly foolish. I know that people have hardly been able to contain their laughter when in a study circle, during the reading from the nature philosopher, Oken, the following sentence occurred : "The human tongue is a cuttle fish." Whatever could he have meant? Of course in actual fact this statement of Oken's can no longer be regarded as correct, but it contains an underlying principle which must be taken into account. When we observe the different animal forms, from the smallest protozoa up to the fully developed apes, we find that every animal form represents some part of the human being, a human organ, or an organic system, which is developed in a one-sided way. You need only look at these things quite crudely. Imagine that the human forehead were to recede enormously that the jaw were to jut right out, that the eyes were to look upwards instead of forwards, that the teeth and their whole nexus were also to be formed in a completely one-sided way. By imagining such an exaggerated, one-sided development you could get a picture of a great variety of mammals. By leaving out this or that in the human form you can change it into the form of an ox, a sheep and so on. And when you take the inner organs, for instance those which are connected with

6—HVIE * *

reproduction, you come into the region of the lower animals. The human being is a synthesis, a putting together of the single animal forms, which becomes softer, gentler, when they are united. The human being is made up of all the animal forms moulded into one harmonious structure. Thus when I trace back to their original forms all that in man is merged together I find the whole animal world. Man is a contraction of the whole animal world.

This way of looking at things places us with our soul life once more in a right relationship to the animal world. This has been forgotten, but it is nevertheless true; and as it belongs fundamentally to the principles of evolution it must again be brought to life. And, after having shown the child how the plant belongs to the earth, we must, in so far as it is possible today, proceed at about the 11th year to a consideration of the animal world; and we must do this in such a way that we realise that in its various forms the animal world belongs, strictly speaking, to man himself. Think how the young human being will then stand in his relation to animal and plant. The plants go to the earth, become one with the earth; the animals become one with him! This gives the basis for a true relationship to the world; it places man in a real relationship to the world. This can always be brought to the child in connection with the teaching matter. And if this is done artistically, if we approach the subject in a living way, so that it corresponds with what the child in his inner being is able to grasp, then we give him living forces with which to establish a relationship to life. Otherwise we may easily destroy this relationship. But we must look deeply into the whole human being.

What really is the etheric body? Well, if it were possible to lift it out of the physical body and so impregnate it that its form were to become visible—then there would be no greater work of art than this. For the human etheric body through its own nature and through what man creates within it, is at one and the same time both work of art and artist. And when we introduce the formative element into the child's artistic work, when we let him model in the free way I described yesterday, we bring to him something that is deeply related to the etheric body. This enables the child to take hold of his own inner being and thereby place himself as man in a right relationship to the world.

By introducing the child to music we form the astral body. But when we put two things together, when we lead what is plastic over into movement, and when we form movements that are plastic, then we have eurythmy, which follows exactly the relationship of the child's etheric body to his astral body. And so now the child learns eurythmy, speech revealing itself in articulated gestures, just as he learned to speak quite naturally in his earlier years. A healthy child will find no difficulty in learning eurythmy, for in eurythmy he simply expresses his own being, he has the impulses to make his own being a reality. This is why, in addition to gymnastics, eurythmy is incorporated into the curriculum as an obligatory subject from the first school years right up into the highest classes.

So you see, eurythmy has arisen out of the whole human being, physical body, etheric body and astral body; it can only be studied by means of an anthroposophical knowledge of man. Gymnastics today are directed physiologically in a one-sided way towards the physical body; and because physiology cannot do otherwise, certain principles based on life-giving processes are introduced. By means of gymnastics, however, we do not educate the complete human being, but only part of him. By saying this nothing is implied against gymnastics, only in these days their importance is over-estimated. Therefore in education today eurythmy should stand side by side with gymnastics. I would not go as far as a famous physiologist did, who once happened to be in the audience when I was speaking about eurythmy. On that occasion I said that as a means of education gymnastics are over-rated at the present time, and that a form of gymnastics calling on the forces of soul and spirit, such as is practised in eurythmy side by side with the study of eurythmy as an art, must be introduced in addition to gymnastics as usually understood. At the end of my lecture the famous

physiologist came up to me and said : Do you say that gymnastics may have their justification as a means of education
because physiologists say so? I, as a physiologist, must say that
gymnastics as a means of education are nothing less than
barbarism ! You would certainly be very astonished if I were to
tell you the name of this physiologist. At the present time such
things are already apparent to people who have some right to
speak; and we must be careful not to advocate certain things in
a fanatical way without a full knowledge of what is involved.
To stand up fanatically for certain things is utterly out of place
in connection with the art of education, because here we are
dealing with the manifold aspects of life.

When we approach the other subjects which children have to
be taught and do so from the various points of view which have
here been considered, we come first to the years during which
the child can only take in the pictorial through his life of
feeling. History and geography, for instance, must be taught in
this way. History must be described pictorially; we must paint
and model with our words. This develops the child's mind. For
during the first two stages of the second main epoch of life
there is one thing above all to which the child has no relationship and this is what may be termed the concept of causation.
Before the 7th year the child should most certainly not go to
school.* If we take the time from 7 to $9\frac{1}{3}$ years old we have
the first subdivision of the second main epoch; from $9\frac{1}{3}$ to $11\frac{2}{3}$
years old we have the second stage and from $11\frac{2}{3}$ until approximately the age of 14 we have the third stage. During the first
stage of this second main epoch the child is so organised that he
responds immediately to what is pictorial. At this age therefore
we must speak as one does in fairy-tales, for everything must
still be undifferentiated from the child's own nature. The plants
must speak with one another, the minerals must speak with one
another; the plants must kiss one another, they must have
father and mother, and so on. At about $9\frac{1}{3}$ years old the time
has come which I have already characterised, when the ego
begins to differentiate itself from the outer world. Then we can

* i.e. to school as distinguished from a kindergarten.

make a more realistic approach in our teaching about plants and animals. Always, however, in the first years of life history must be treated in fairy-tale, mythical mood. In the second subdivision of this longer epoch, that is to say, from $9\frac{1}{3}$ until $11\frac{2}{3}$ years old, we must speak pictorially. And only when the child approaches the age of 12 can one introduce him to the concept of causation, only then can one lead over to abstract concepts, whereby cause and effect can be allowed to enter in. Before this time the child is as inaccessible to cause and effect as anyone colour blind is to colours; and as an educator one often has absolutely no idea how unnecessary it is to speak to the child about cause and effect. It is only after the age of 12 that we can speak to him about things which today are taken for granted when looked at from a scientific point of view.

This makes it essential to wait until about the 12th year before dealing with anything that has to do with the lifeless, for this involves entering into the concept of causation. And in the teaching of history we must also wait until about this age before passing over from a pictorial presentation to one which deals with cause and effect, where the causes underlying historical events have to be sought. Before this we should only concern ourselves with what can be brought to the child as having life, soul-imbued life.

People are really very strange. For instance, in the course of cultural development a concept has arisen which goes by the name of animism. It is maintained that when a child knocks himself against a table he imagines the table to be alive and hits it. He dreams a soul into the table, and it is thought that primitive people did the same. The idea is prevalent that something very complicated takes place in the soul of the child. He is supposed to think that the table is alive, ensouled, and this is why he hits it when he bumps up against it. This is a fantastic notion. On the contrary those who study the history of culture are the ones who do actually "ensoul" something, for they "ensoul" this imaginative capacity into the child. But the soul qualities of the child are far more deeply embedded in the physical body than they are later, when they are emancipated and can work freely. When the child bumps against a table a reflex action is set up without his imagining that the table is alive. It is purely a reflex movement of will, for the child does not yet differentiate himself from the outer world. This differentiation first makes its appearance at about the 12th year when a healthy child can grasp the concept of causation. But when this concept is brought to the child too early, especially if it is done by means of crude external methods, really terrible conditions are set up in the child's development. It is all very well to say that one should take pains to make everything perfectly clear to a child. Calculating machines already exist in which little balls are pushed here and there in order to make the operations of arithmetic externally obvious. The next thing we may expect is that those of the same frame of mind will make moral concepts externally visible by means of some kind of machine in which by pushing something about one will be able to see good and evil in the same way as with the calculating machines one can see that 5 plus 7 equals 12. There are, however, undoubtedly spheres of life in which things cannot be made externally apparent and which are taken up and absorbed by the child in ways that are not at all obvious; and we greatly err if we try to make them so. Hence it is quite wrong to do as is often attempted in educational books and make externally apparent what by its very nature cannot be so treated. In this respect people often fall into really frightful trivialities.

In the years between the change of teeth and puberty we are not only concerned with the demonstrably obvious, for when we take the whole of human life into consideration the following becomes clear. At the age of 8 I take in some concept, I do not yet understand it fully; indeed I do not understand it at all as far as its abstract content is concerned. I am not yet so constituted as to make this possible. Why then do I take in the concept at all? I do so because it is my teacher who is speaking, because the authority of my teacher is self-understood and this works upon me. But today we are not supposed to do this; the child is to be shown what is visual and obvious. Now let us take

a child who is taught everything in this way. In such a case
what a child experiences does not grow with his growth, for by
these methods he is treated as a being who does not grow. But
we should not awaken in the child ideas which cannot grow
with him, for then we should be doing the same thing as if we
were to have a pair of shoes made for a three-year-old child
and expect him to wear them when he is 12. Everything in the
human being grows, including his power of comprehension; and
so the concepts must grow with him. We must therefore see to
it that we bring living concepts to the child, but this we can
only do if there is a living relationship to the authority of the
teacher. It is not achieved if the teacher is an abstract pedant
who stands in front of the child and presents him with concepts
which are as yet totally foreign to him. Picture two children.
One has been taught in such a way that he takes in concepts
and at the age of 45 he still gives things the same explanation
that he learned when he was 8 years old. The concept has not
grown with the child; he paid careful attention to it all, and at
45 can still explain it in the same way. Now let us take a
second child who has been educated in a living way. Here we
shall find that just as he no longer wears the same size shoes as
he did when he was 8 years old, so at a later age he no longer
carries around with him the same concepts that he learned
when he was 8. On the contrary; these concepts have expanded
and have become something quite different. All this reacts on
the physical body. And if we look at these two people in regard
to their physical fitness we find that the first man has sclerosis
at the age of 45, while the second has remained mobile and is
not sclerotic. How great do you think the differences are which
come to light between human beings? In a certain place in
Europe there were once two professors of philosophy. One was
famous for his Greek philosophy; the other was an old
Hegelian, an adherent of the school of Hegel, where people
were still accustomed to take in living concepts, even after the
age of 20. Both were lecturers at the same university. At the
age of 70 the first decided to exercise his right to retire on a
pension, he felt unable to continue. The second, the Hegelian

professor, was 91 and said : "I cannot understand why that young fellow is settling down to retirement already." But the conceptual life of this second professor had retained its mobility. People criticised him for this very reason and accused him of being inconsistent. The other man was consistent, but he suffered from sclerosis!

There exists a complete unity in the child between the spiritual and the bodily, and we can only deal rightly with him when we take this into consideration. Today people who do not share the views of materialists say that materialism is a bad thing. Why? Many will say that it is bad because it understands nothing of the spiritual. This, however, is not the worst, for little by little people will become aware of this lack, and as a result of the urge to get the better of it they will come to the spiritual. The worst thing about materialism is that it understands nothing of matter! Look into it yourselves and see what has become of the knowledge of the living forces of man in lung, liver and so on under the influences of materialism. Nothing is known about how these things work. A portion is removed from the lung, the liver and so forth and this is prepared and examined, but by means of present-day scientific methods nothing is learned of the spirit working actively in the human organs. Such knowledge can only be gained through spiritual science. The material reveals its nature only when studied from the aspect of spiritual science. Materialism has fallen sick, and the cause of this sickness is above all because the materialist understands nothing of matter. He wants to limit himself to what is material but he cannot penetrate to any knowledge of what is material in a real sense. In saying this I do not mean the "thought-out" material, where so and so many atoms are supposed to dance around a central nucleus : for things of this kind are not difficult to construct. In the earlier days of the Theosophical Society there were theosophists who constructed a whole system based on atoms and molecules; but it was all just thought out. What we have to do now is to approach reality once again. And if one actually does this one has a feeling of discomfort when one is supposed to grasp some concept which is entirely devoid of reality. One experiences pain when, for instance, someone propounds a theory such as this : Fundamentally it is one and the same thing whether I drive my car to a town, or whether the car stands still and the town comes to me. Certainly things of this kind are justified when looked at from a certain point of view. But drawn out to the extent that occurs today among those who hold completely abstract opinions, they impoverish the entire life of the human soul. And anyone who has a sense for such things experiences great pain in regard to much of what people think today, which works so destructively on teaching methods. For instance, I see the tendencies of certain methods applied already to little children in the kindergarten, who are given ordinary cut-out letters and then learn to pick them out of a heap and put them together to form words. By occupying the child in this way at such an early age we are bringing him something to which as yet he has absolutely no relationship. When this happens to him the effect is the same as if in real thinking one were to say : I was once a man who still had muscles, skin and so on; now I am merely a skeleton. So it is today under the influence of this propensity for abstractions in the spiritual life of mankind : one sees oneself suddenly as a skeleton. With such an outlook, however, which is the bare skeleton of reality, we cannot approach the child in education.

Because of this I wanted to show today how everything depends on the teacher approaching life in a true and living way.

LECTURE V

Arnheim, 21st July, 1924

At this point of our educational studies I want to interpolate some remarks referring to the arrangements which were made in the Waldorf School in order to facilitate and put into practice those principles about which I have already spoken and shall have more to say in the coming lectures.

The Waldorf School in Stuttgart was inaugurated in the year 1919 on the initiative of Emil Molt,* with the purpose of carrying out the principles of anthroposophical education. This purpose could be realised through the fact that the direction and leadership of the school was entrusted to me. Therefore when I describe how this school is organised it can at the same time serve as an example for the practical realisation of those fundamental educational principles which we have been dealing with here.

I should like to make clear first of all that the soul of all the instruction and education in the Waldorf School is the Teachers' Conference. These conferences are held regularly by the college of teachers and I attend them whenever I can manage to be in Stuttgart. They are concerned not only with external matters of school organisation, with the drawing up of the timetable, with the formation of classes and so on, but they deal in a penetrative, far-reaching way with everything on which the life and soul of the school depends. Things are arranged in such a way as to further the aim of the school, that is to say, to base the teaching and education on a knowledge of man. It means of course that this knowledge must be applied to every individual child. Time must be devoted to the observation, the psychological observation of each child. This is

* Director of the Waldorf-Astoria cigarette factory.

essential and must be reckoned with in actual, concrete detail when building up the whole educational plan. In the teachers' conferences the individual child is spoken about in such a way that the teachers try to grasp the nature of the human being as such in its special relationship to the child in question. You can well imagine that we have to deal with all grades and types of children with their varying childish talents and qualities of soul. We are confronted with pretty well every kind of child, from the one whom we must class as being psychologically and physically very poorly endowed to the one —and let us hope life will confirm this—who is gifted to the point of genius.

If we want to observe children in their real being we must acquire a psychological faculty of perception. This kind of perception not only includes a cruder form of observing the capacities of individual children, but above all the ability to appraise these capacities rightly. You need only consider the following : One can have a child in the class who appears to be extraordinarily gifted in learning to read and write, or seems to be very gifted in learning arithmetic or languages. But to hold fast to one's opinion and say : This child is gifted, for he can learn languages, arithmetic and so on quite easily—this betokens a psychological superficiality. In childhood, say at about 7, 8 or 9 years old the ease with which a child learns can be a sign that later on he will develop genius; but it can equally well be a sign that sooner or later he will become neurotic, or in some way turn into a sick man. When one has gained insight into the human being and knows that this human being consists not only of the physical body which is perceptible to the eye, but also bears within him the etheric body which is the source of growth and the forces of nourishment, the cause whereby the child grows bigger; when one considers further that man also has an astral body within him, the laws of which have nothing whatever to do with what is being physically established but on the contrary work destructively on the physical, and destroy it in order to make room for the spiritual; and furthermore when one considers that there is still the ego-organisation which is bound up with the human being, so that one has the three organisations—etheric body, astral body, ego-organisation and must pay heed to these as well as to the perceptible physical body—then one can form an idea of how complicated such a human being is, and how each of these members of the human being can be the cause of a talent, or lack of talent in any particular sphere, or can show a deceptive talent which is transient and pathological. One must develop insight as to whether the talent is of such a kind as to have healthy tendencies, or whether it tends towards the unhealthy.

If as teacher and educator, one represents with the necessary love, devotion and selflessness the knowledge of man of which we have been speaking here in these lectures, then something very definite ensues. In living together with the children one becomes—do not misunderstand the word, it is not used in a bragging sense—one becomes ever wiser and wiser. One discovers for oneself how to appraise some particular capacity or achievement of the child. One learns to enter in a living way into the nature of the child and to do so comparatively quickly.

I know that many people will say: If you assert that the human being, in addition to his physical body, consists of supersensible members, etheric body, astral body and ego-organisation, it follows that only someone who is clairvoyant and able to perceive these supersensible members of human nature can be a teacher. But this is not the case. Everything perceived through imagination, inspiration and intuition, as described in my books, can be examined and assessed by observing the physical organisation of the child, because it comes to expression everywhere in this physical organisation.

It is therefore perfectly possible for a teacher or educator who carries out his profession in a truly loving way and bases his teaching on a comprehensive knowledge of man, to speak in the following way about some special case : Here the physical body shows signs of hardening, of stiffening, so that the child is unable to develop the faculties which, spiritually, are potentially present, because the physical body is a hindrance. Or, to take another case, it is possible that someone might say : In

this particular child, who is about 7 or 8 years old, certain
attributes are making their appearance. The child surprises
us in that he is able to learn this or that very early; but one can
observe that the physical body is too soft, it has a tendency
which later on may cause it to run to fat. If the physical body
is too soft, if, so to say, the fluid element has an excess of
weight in relation to the solid element, then this particular
tendency causes the soul and spirit to make themselves felt
too soon, and then we have a precocious child. In such a
case, during the further development of the physical body,
this precocity is pushed back again, so that under certain
conditions everything may well be changed and the child
become for the whole of life, not only an average person, but
one even below average. In short, we must reckon with the
fact that what external observation reveals in the child must
be estimated rightly by means of inner perceptiveness, so that
actually nothing whatever is said if one merely speaks about
faculties or lack of faculties.

What I am now saying can also be borne out by studying
the biographies of the most varied types of human being. In
following the course of the spiritual development of mankind
it would be possible to cite many a distinguished personality
who in later life achieved great things, but who was regarded
as a child as being almost completely ungifted and at school
had been, so to say, one of the duffers. In this connection one
comes across the most remarkable examples. For instance there
is a poet who at the age of 18, 19 and even 20 was held to be
so ungifted by all those who were concerned with his education that they advised him, for this very reason, not to
attempt studying at a higher level. He did not, however, allow
himself to be put off, but continued his studies, and it was not
so long afterwards that he was appointed inspector of the very
same schools that it had not been thought advisable for him to
attend as a young man. There was also an Austrian poet,
Robert Hamerling, who studied with the purpose of becoming
a teacher in a secondary school (Gymnasium). In the examination he obtained excellent marks for Greek and Latin; on the

other hand he did not pass muster for the teaching of the German language, because his essays were considered to be quite inadequate. Nevertheless he became a famous poet! We have found it necessary to separate a number of children from the others, either more or less permanently or for a short time, because they are mentally backward and through their lack of comprehension, through their inability to understand, they are a cause of disturbance. These children are put together into a special class for those who are of limited capacity. This class is led by the man who has spoken to you here, Dr. Schubert, whose very special qualities make him a born leader of such a class. This task calls indeed for special gifts. It needs above all the gift of being able to penetrate into those qualities of soul which are, as it were, imprisoned in the physical and have difficulty in freeing themselves. Little by little they must be liberated. Here we come again to what borders on physical illness, where the psychologically abnormal impinges on what is physically out of order. It is quite possible to shift this borderland, it is in no way rigid or fixed. Indeed it is certainly helpful if one can look behind every so-called psychological abnormality and perceive what is not healthy in the physical organism of the person in question. For in the true sense of the word there are no mental illnesses; they are brought about through the fact that the physical does not release the spiritual.

In Germany today* we have also to reckon with the situation that nearly all school children are not only under-nourished, but have suffered for years from the effects of undernourishment. Here therefore we are concerned with the fact that through observing the soul-spiritual and the physical-corporeal we can be led to a comprehension of their essential unity. People find it very difficult to understand that this is essential in education. There was an occasion when a man, who otherwise was possessed of considerable understanding and was directly engaged in matters pertaining to schools, visited the Waldorf School. I myself took him around for days on end.

* Just after the First World War.

He showed great interest in everything. But after I had told him all I could about one child or another—for we spoke mostly about the children, not about abstract educational principles, our education being based on a knowledge of man—he finally said : "Well and good, but then all teachers would have to be doctors." I replied : "That is not necessary; but they should certainly have some medical knowledge, as much as a teacher needs to know for his educational work."

For where shall we be if it is said that for some reason or another, provision cannot be made for it, or the teachers cannot learn it? Provision simply must be made for what is required and the teachers must learn what is necessary. This is the only possible standpoint. The so-called normal capacities which man develops, which are present in every human being, are best studied by observing pathological conditions. And if one has learned to know a sick organism from various points of view, then the foundation is laid for understanding a soul endowed with genius. It is not as though I were taking the standpoint of a Lombroso* or someone holding similar views; this is not the case. I do not assert that genius is always a condition of sickness, but one does actually learn to know the soul-spiritual in learning to know the sick body of a child. In studying the difficulties experienced by soul and spirit in coming to outer manifestation in a sick body, one can learn to understand how the soul seizes hold of the organism when it has something special to express.

So education comes up against not only slight pathological conditions, such as are present in children of limited capacity, but it meets what is pathological in the widest sense of the word. This is why we have also introduced medical treatment for the children in our school. We do not, however, have a doctor who only practises medicine and is quite outside the sphere of education, but our school doctor, Dr. Kolisko, is at the same time the teacher of a class. He stands completely within the school as a teacher, he is acquainted with all the

* Italian criminologist.

children and is therefore in a position to know the particular angle from which may come any pathological symptom appearing in the child. This is altogether different from what is possible for the school doctor who visits the school on certain formal occasions and judges the state of a child's health on what is necessarily a very cursory observation. Quite apart from this, however, in the teachers' conferences no hard and fast line is drawn between the soul-spiritual and physical-corporeal when considering the case of any particular child. The natural consequence of this is that the teacher has gradually to acquire insight into the whole human being, so that he is just as interested in every detail connected with physical health and sickness as he is in what is mentally sound or abnormal.

This is what we try to achieve in the school. Each teacher should have the deepest interest in, and pay the greatest attention to the whole human being. It follows from this that our teachers are not specialists in the ordinary sense of the word. For in effect the point is not so much whether the history teacher is more or less master of his subject, but whether by and large he is the kind of personality who is able to work upon the children in the way that has been described, and whether he has an awareness of how the child is developing under his care.

I myself was obliged to teach from my 15th year onwards, simply in order to live. I had to give private lessons and so gained direct experience in the practice of education and teaching. For instance, when I was a very young man, only 21, I undertook the education of a family of four boys. I became resident in the family, and at that time one of the boys was 11 years old and he was clearly hydrocephalic. He had most peculiar habits. He disliked eating at table, and would leave the dining room and go into the kitchen where there were the bins for refuse and scraps. There he would eat not only potato peelings but also all the other mess thrown there. At 11 years old he still knew practically nothing. An attempt had been made, on the basis of earlier instruction which he had received, to let him sit for the entrance examination to a primary school, in the hope that he could be received into one of the classes. But when he handed in the results of the examination there was nothing but an exercise book with one large hole where he had rubbed something out. He had achieved nothing else whatever and he was already 11 years old. The parents were distressed. They belonged to the more cultured upper-middle class, and everybody said: The boy is abnormal. Naturally when such things are said about a child people feel a prejudice against him. The general opinion was that he must learn a trade, for he was capable of nothing else. I came into the family, but nobody really understood me when I stated what I was prepared to do. I said: If I am given complete responsibility for the boy I can promise nothing except that I will try to draw out of the boy what is in him. Nobody understood this except the mother, with her instinctive perception, and the excellent family doctor. It was the same doctor who later on, together with Dr. Freud, founded psycho-analysis. When, however, at a later stage it became decadent, he severed his connection with it. It was possible to talk with this man and our conversation led to the decision that I should be entrusted with the boy's education and training.

In eighteen months his head had become noticeably smaller and the boy was now sufficiently advanced to enter a secondary school (Gymnasium). I accompanied him further during his school career for he needed extra help, but nevertheless after eighteen months he was accepted as a pupil in a secondary school. To be sure, his education had to be carried on in such a way that there were times when I needed $1\frac{1}{2}$ hours in order to prepare what I wanted the boy to learn in a quarter of an hour. It was essential to exercise the greatest economy when teaching him and never to spend more time on whatever it might be than was absolutely necessary. It was also a question of arranging the day's timetable with great exactitude: so much time must be given to music, so much to gymnastics, so much to going for walks and so on. If this is done, I said to myself, if the boy is educated in this way, then it will be possible to draw out of him what is latent within him. Now there were times when things went quite badly with my efforts in this direction. The boy became pale. With the exception of his mother and the family doctor people said with one accord : That fellow is ruining the boy's health !—To this I replied : Naturally I cannot continue with his education if there is any interference. Things must be allowed to go on according to our agreement. And they went on.

The boy went through secondary school, continued his studies and became a doctor. The only reason for his early death was that when he was called up and served as a doctor during the world war he caught an infection and died of the effects of the ensuing illness. But he carried out the duties of his medical profession in an admirable way. I only bring forward this example in order to show how necessary it is in education to see things all round, as a whole. It also shows how under certain definite educational treatment it is possible in the long run to reduce week by week a hydrocephalic condition.

Now you will say : Certainly, something of this kind can happen when it is a case of private tuition. But it can equally well happen with comparatively large classes. For anyone who enters lovingly into what is put forward here as the knowledge of man will quickly acquire the possibility of observing each individual child with the attention that is necessary; and this he will be able to do even in a class where there are many pupils. It is just here however that the psychological perception of the kind which I have described is necessary, but this perception is not so easily acquired if one goes through the world as a single individual and has absolutely no interest in other people. I can truly say that I am aware of what I owe to the fact that I really never found any human being uninteresting. Even as a child no human being was ever uninteresting to me. And I know that I should never have been able to educate that boy if I had not actually found all human beings interesting.

It is this width of interest which permeates the teachers' conferences at the Waldorf School and gives them atmosphere, so that—if I may so express myself—a psychological mood prevails throughout and these teachers' conferences then really become a school based on the study of a deep psychology. It is interesting to see how from year to year the "college of teachers" as a whole is able to deepen its faculty for psychological perception. In addition to all that I have already described, the following must also be stated when one comes to consider the individual classes. We do not go in for statistics in the ordinary sense of the word, but for us the classes are living beings also, not only the individual pupils. One can take some particular class and study it for itself, and it is extraordinarily interesting to observe what imponderable forces then come to light. When one studies such a class, and when the teachers of the different classes discuss in college meeting the special characteristics of each class, it is interesting for instance to discover that a class having in it more girls than boys—for ours is a co-educational school—is a completely different being from a class where there are more boys than girls; and a class consisting of an equal number of boys and girls is again a completely different being. All this is extremely interesting, not only on account of the talk which takes place among the children, nor of the little love affairs which always occur in the higher classes. Here one must acquire the right kind of observation in order to take notice of it when this is necessary and otherwise not to see it. Quite apart from this however is the fact that the imponderable "being" composed of the different masculine and feminine individuals gives the class a quite definite spiritual structure. In this way one learns to know the individuality of the different classes. And if, as with us in the Waldorf School, there are parallel classes, it is possible when necessary—it is very seldom necessary—to make some alteration in the division of the classes. Studies such as these, in connection with the classes, form ever and again the content of the teachers' conferences. Thus the content of these conferences does not consist only of the administration of the school, but provides a living continuation of education in the school itself, so that the teachers are always learning. In this way the conferences are the soul of the whole school. One learns to estimate trivialities rightly, to give due weight to what has real importance, and so on. Then there will not be an outcry when here or there a child commits some small misdemeanour; but there will be an awareness when something happens which might endanger the further development of the school. So the total picture of our Waldorf School which has only come about in the course of the years, is an interesting one. By and large our children, when they reach the higher classes, are more able to grasp what a child has to learn at school than those from other schools; on the other hand, as I have described, in the lower classes they remain somewhat behind in reading and writing because we use different methods which are extended over several years. Between the ages of 13 and 15, however, the children begin to outstrip the pupils of other schools owing, among other things, to a certain ease with which they are able to enter into things and to a certain aptness of comprehension.

Now a great difficulty arises. It is a remarkable fact that where there is a light, shadows are thrown by objects; where there is a weak light there are weak shadows, where there is a strong light there are strong shadows. Likewise in regard to certain qualities of soul, the following may be observed. If insufficient care is taken by the teachers to establish contact with their pupils in every possible way, so that they are models on which the children base their own behaviour, then, conversely, as the result of a want of contact it can easily happen that deviations from moral conduct make their appearance. About this we must have no illusions whatever. It is so. This is why so much depends upon a complete "growing together" of the individualities of the teachers and the individualities of the pupils, so that the strong inner attachment felt by the children for the teachers on the one side may be reciprocally experienced by the teachers on the other, thus assuring the further development of both.

These things need to be studied in an inner, human, loving way, otherwise one will meet with surprises. But the nature of the method is such that it tends to draw out everything that lies potentially in the human being. At times this is exemplified in a somewhat strange fashion. There is a German poet who knew that he had been badly brought up and badly taught, so that very many of his innate qualities—he was always complaining about this—could not come to expression. This was because his body had already become stiff and hardened, owing to the fact that in his youth no care had been taken to develop his individuality. Then one day he went to a phrenologist. Do not imagine that I am standing up for phrenology or that I rate it particularly highly; it has however some significance when practised intuitively. The phrenologist felt his head and told him all kinds of nice things, for these were of course to be found; but at one spot of the skull he stopped suddenly, became red and did not trust himself to say a word. The poet then said : "Come now, speak out, that is the predisposition to theft in me. It seems therefore that if I had been better educated at school this tendency to theft might have had very serious consequences."

If we wish to educate we must have plenty of elbow room. This however is not provided for in a school which is run on ordinary lines according to the dreadful timetable : 8 to 9 religion, 9 to 10 gymnastics, 10 to 11 history, 11 to 12 arithmetic. What comes later blots out what has been given earlier, and as, in spite of this, one has to get results, a teacher is wellnigh driven to despair. This is why in the Waldorf School we have what may be termed teaching *periods*. The child comes into a class. Every day during Main Lesson, which continues for the best part of the morning, from 8 to 10 or from 8 to 11, with short breaks for recreation, he is taught one subject. This is given by *one* teacher, even in the higher classes. The subject is not changed hour by hour, but is continued for as long as may be necessary for the teacher to get through what he wishes to take with the class. In arithmetic, for instance, such a period might last 4 weeks. Every day then, from 8 to 10 the subject in question is carried further and what is given one day is linked on to what was taught the previous day. No later lesson blots out the one given earlier; concentration is possible. Then, after about 4 weeks, when the arithmetic period has been taken far enough and is brought to a conclusion, a history period may follow, and this again, according to the length of time required, will be continued for another 4 or 5 weeks. And so it goes on. Our point of view is the very opposite to what is called the system of the specialist teacher. You might for instance when visiting the Waldorf School find our Dr. Baravalle taking a class for descriptive geometry. The pupils sit facing him with their drawing boards in front of them. He lets them draw and his manner is that of the most exemplary specialist teacher of geometry. Now coming into another school and looking at its list of professors and teachers you will find appended to one name or another : Diploma in Geometry or Mathematics or whatever it may be. I have known very many teachers, specialists in mathematics for instance, who boasted of the fact that when they took part in a school outing they were quite unable to tell the children the names of the plants.—But morning school is not yet over and here you will see Dr. Baravalle walking up and down between the desks and giving an English lesson. And out of the whole manner and method of his teaching you will see that he is speaking about all kinds of things and there is no means of knowing in which subject he is a specialist. Some of you may think geography is his special subject, or geometry or something else. The essential substance and content of one's teaching material can undoubtedly be acquired very quickly if one has the gift of entering right into the sphere of cognition, of experiencing knowledge within the soul. So we have no timetable. Naturally there is nothing pedantic about this. In our Waldorf School the Main Lesson is given in periods; other lessons must of course be fitted into a timetable, but these follow on after the Main Lesson.

Then we think it very important that the children should be taught two foreign languages from the time they first come to school when they are still quite small. We take French and English. It must be admitted that in our school this can be a perfect misery, because so many pupils have joined the school since its foundation. For instance pupils came to us who should really be taken into Class 6. In this class however, there are children who have already made considerable progress in languages. Now these new children should join them, but they have to be put into Class 5 simply because they haven't the foggiest notion of languages. We have continually to reckon with the difficulties.

Another thing we try to arrange is that whenever possible the most fundamental lessons are given in the morning, so that physical training—gymnastics, eurythmy and so on—is kept for the afternoon. This however is no hard and fast arrangement, for as we cannot afford an endless number of teachers not everything can be fitted in as ideally as we would wish, but only as well as circumstances permit. You will not misunderstand me if I say that with ideals no beginning can be made. Do not say that anthroposophy is not idealistic. We know how to value ideals, but nothing can be begun with ideals. They can be beautifully described, one can say : This is how it ought to be. One can even flatter oneself that one is striving in this direction. But in reality we have to cope with a quite definite, concrete school made up of 800 children whom we know and with between 40 and 50 teachers whom we must also know. But what is the use (you may ask) of a college of teachers when no member of it corresponds to the ideal? The essential thing is that we reckon with what is there. Then we proceed in accordance with reality. If we want to carry out something practically we must take reality into account. This then is what I would say in regard to period teaching.

Owing to our free approach to teaching, and this must certainly be apparent from what I am describing to you, it naturally comes about that the children do not always sit as still as mice. But you should see how the whole moral atmosphere and inner constitution of a class depends on the one who has it in charge, and here again it is the imponderable that counts. In this connection I must say that in the Waldorf School there are also teachers who prove to be inadequate in certain respects. I will not describe them, but it can well happen that on entering a class one is aware that it is "out of tune". A quarter of the class is lying under the benches, a quarter is on top of them and the rest are continually running out of the room and knocking on the door from outside. We must not let these things baffle us. The situation can be put right again if one knows how to get on with the children. They should be allowed to satisfy their urge for movement; one should not fall back on punishment but set about putting these things right in another way. We are not at all in favour of issuing commands; on the contrary with us everything must be allowed to develop by itself. Through this very fact however there also develops by itself what I have described as something lying within the teachers as their life. Certainly the children sometimes make a frightful noise, but this is only a sign of their vitality. They can also be very active and lively in doing what they should, provided the teacher knows how to arouse their interest. We must of course make use of the good qualities of the so-called good child, so that he learns something, and with a rascal we must even make use of his rascally qualities, so that he too makes progress. We do not get anywhere if we are only able to develop the good qualities. We must from time to time develop the so-called rascally qualities, only we must of course be able to turn them in the right direction. Very often these so-called rascally qualities are precisely those which signify strength in the grown-up human being; they are qualities which, rightly handled, can culminate in what is most excellent in the grown up man or woman.

And so ever and again one has to determine whether a child gives little trouble because he is good, or because he is ill. It is very easy, if one considers one's own convenience, to be just as pleased with the sick child who sits still and does not make himself heard, as with the good child, because he does not call for much attention. But if one looks with real penetration into human nature one often finds that one has to devote much more attention to such a child than to a so-called rascal. Here too it is a question of psychological insight and psychological treatment, the latter naturally from the soul-spiritual point of view.

There is another thing to be considered. In the Waldorf School practically all the teaching takes place in the school itself. The burden of homework is lifted, for the children are

given very little to do at home. Because of this, because all the
work is done together with the teachers, the children's attitude
is a quite remarkable one. In the Waldorf School something
very characteristic comes about, as the following example will
show : There was an occasion when certain pupils had mis-
behaved. A teacher who was not yet fully permeated with the
Waldorf School education felt it necessary to punish these
children and he did so in an intellectualistic way. He said :
"You must stay in after school and do some arithmetic." The
children were quite unable to understand that doing arithmetic
could be regarded as a punishment, for this was something
which gave them the greatest pleasure. And the whole class—
this is something which actually happened—asked : "May we
stay in too?" And this was intended as a punishment ! You see,
the whole attitude of mind changes completely, and it should
never happen that a child feels that he is being punished when
he has to do something which he actually does with devotion,
with satisfaction and joy. Our teachers discover all sorts of ways
of getting rid of wrong behaviour. Once it so happened that
our Dr. Stein, who is particularly inventive in this respect,
noticed that during his lesson in a higher class the children were
writing letters and passing them round. Now what did he do in
order to put the matter right? He began to speak about the
postal service, explaining it in some detail and in such a way
that the writing of letters gradually ceased. The description of
the postal service, the history of the origin of correspondence
had apparently nothing to do with the misdemeanour noticed
by the teacher and nevertheless it had something to do with it.
You see, if one does not ask in a rationalistic way : "What shall
I do" but is able to take advantage of a sudden idea because
one knows instinctively how to deal with any situation in class,
the consequences are often good; for in this way much more
can be achieved towards the correction of the pupils than by
resorting to punishment.

It must above all be clear to every member of the class that
the teacher himself truly lives in accordance with his precepts.
It must never come about that a choleric boy who makes a

mess of his exercise books, seizes his neighbour by the ears and tweaks his hair, is shouted at by the teacher : "How dare you lose your temper, how dare you behave in such a way ! Boy, if you ever repeat such a performance I will hurl the inkpot at your head !" This is certainly radically described, but something of the kind may well happen if a teacher does not realise that he himself must be an example in the school of what he expects of the pupils. What one is has far more importance than having principles and a lot of knowledge. What kind of a person one is, that is the point. If a candidate in the examination for teachers, in which he is supposed to show that he is well-fitted for his calling, is only tested in what he knows, —well, what he knows in the examination room is precisely what later on he will have to look up again in his text books. But this can be done without the need of sitting for an examination. But in actual fact no one should enter a school who has not the individuality of a teacher, in body, soul and spirit. Because this is so I can say that in carrying out my task of choosing the teachers comprising the College of Teachers at the Waldorf School, I certainly do not regard it as an obstacle if someone has obtained his teacher's diploma, but in certain respects I look more closely at one who has passed his examination than at another who through his purely human attitude shows me that his individuality is that of a true teacher. It is always a matter of concern when someone has passed examinations; he can undoubtedly still be an extremely clever man, but this must be in spite of having passed examinations.

It is remarkable how Karma works, for the Waldorf School, which is intended to stand as a concrete example of this special education based on the knowledge of man, was actually only possible in Württemberg, nowhere else, because just at the time when we were preparing to open the school a very old school regulation was still in force. If at that time people had been taken hold of by the enlightened ideas which later came forth from the constitutional body of the Weimar National Assembly (Nationalversammlung) with which we have constantly to contend, because it wishes to demolish our lower classes, we should

never have been able to create the Waldorf School. It will
certainly become ever rarer and rarer for teachers to be judged
according to their human individualities and not according to
their qualifications. It will become even rarer in the lower
classes to be able to do this or that; for the world works—how
can one put it—towards "freedom" and "human dignity". This
"human dignity" is however furthered in a strange manner by
the help of the time-table and general arrangement of lessons.
In the capital city of a country there is a Ministry of
Education. In this Ministry it is known what is taught in each
school and class by means of regulations which apportion
exactly how the subjects are to be divided up. The consequence
is that in some out-of-the-way place there is a school. If
information is required as to what exactly is being taught for
instance on 21st July, 1924 at 9.30 a.m. in the 5th class of this
Primary School it has only to be looked up in the corresponding
records of the Ministry and one can say precisely what is being
taught in the school in question.—With us, on the contrary,
you have two parallel classes, 5A and 5B. You go perhaps into
both classes, one after the other and are astonished to find that
in the one parallel class something completely different is going
on from what is happening in the other. There is no similarity.
Classes 5A and 5B are entrusted entirely to the individuality of
the class teacher; each can do what corresponds to his own
individuality, and he does it. In spite of the fact that in the
teachers' conferences there is absolute agreement on essential
matters, there is no obligation for the one class to be taught in
just the same way as the parallel class; for what we seek to
achieve must be achieved in the most varied ways. It is never a
question of external regulations. So you will find with the little
children in Class 1 that a teacher may do something of this
kind* in order to help the children to find their way into
drawing with paintbrush and paint : you come into the class
and see the children making all kinds of movements with their
hands which will then be led over to mastering the use of brush
or pencil. Or you come into the other class and there you see

* Dr Steiner made movements with his hands.

the children dancing around in order that the same skill may be
drawn out of the movement of the legs. Each teacher does what
he deems to be best suited to the individualities of the children
and his own individuality. In this way life is brought into the
class and already forms the basis of what makes the children
feel that they really belong to their teachers.

Naturally, in spite of that old school regulation, in
Württemberg, too, there is school inspection; but in regard to
this we have come off quite well. The inspectors' attitude
showed the greatest possible insight and they agreed to everything when they saw how and why it was done. But such
occasions also give rise to quite special happenings. For
example, the inspectors came into a class where the teacher
usually experienced great difficulty in maintaining discipline.
Time and again she had to break into her teaching and not
without considerable trouble re-establish order. Well, the inspectors from the Ministry came into her class and the teacher was
highly astonished at the perfect behaviour of the children. They
were model pupils, so much so that on the following day she
felt bound to allude to it and said : "Children, how good you
were yesterday !" Thereupon the whole class exclaimed : "But
of course, Fräulein Doktor, we will never let *you* down!"
Something quite imponderable develops in the pupils when the
teachers try to put into practice what I have stated at the
conclusion of all these lectures. If children are taught and
educated in such a way that life is livingly carried over into
their lives, then out of such teaching life-forces develop which
continue to grow and prosper.

LECTURE VI

Arnheim, 22nd July, 1924

Today, before going into any further explanations concerning questions of method, I should like to add something more to what I said yesterday about the teachers' conferences. We attach the greatest importance to our relationship with the parents of our Waldorf School children and in order to ensure complete harmony and agreement we arrange Parents' Evenings fairly frequently, which are attended by parents of children living in the neighbourhood. At these meetings the intentions, methods and the various arrangements of the school are discussed—naturally in a more or less general way—and, in so far as this is possible in such gatherings, the parents have the opportunity of expressing their wishes and these are given a sympathetic hearing. In this way the opportunity is provided actually to work out what we should seek to achieve in our education and moreover to do this in the whole social milieu out of which such aims have in truth their origin. The teachers hear the ideas of the parents in regard to the education of their children; and the parents hear—it is our practice always to speak with the utmost sincerity and candour—about what is taking place in the school, what our thoughts are about the education and future of the children and why it is that we think it necessary to have schools which further a free approach to education. In short, by this means the mutual understanding between teachers and parents is not only of an abstract and intellectual nature, but a continuous human contact is brought about. We feel this contact to be very important, for we have nothing else to depend upon. In a state school, everything is strictly defined. There one knows with absolute certainty the aims which the teacher must bear in mind; he knows for instance, that at 9 years of age a child must have reached a certain standard, and so on. Everything is planned with exactitude.

With us everything depends on the free individuality of each single teacher. In so far as I may be considered the director of the school, nothing is given in the way of rules and regulations. Actually there is no school director in the usual sense, but each teacher reigns supreme. Instead of a school director or headmaster we have the teachers' conferences, in which there is a common study and a common striving towards further progress. There is therefore a spirit, a concrete spirit living among the college of teachers which works freely, which is not tyrannical, which does not issue statements, rules or programmes, but has the will continually to progress, continually to make better and better arrangements, in meeting the teaching requirements. Today our teachers cannot know at all what will be good in the Waldorf School in 5 years time for in these 5 years they will have learned a great deal and out of the knowledge they will have to judge anew what is good and what is not good. This is also the reason why what associations for educational reform decide to be valuable is a matter of complete indifference in the Waldorf School. Educational matters cannot be thought out intellectually, they can only arise out of teaching experience. And it is this working out of experience which is the concern of the college of teachers. But just because we are in this situation, just because we live in a state of flux in regard to what we ourselves actually want, we need a different kind of support than is given to an ordinary school by the educational authorities, who ordain what should be done. We need the support of that social element in which the children are growing up. We need the inner support of the parents in connection with all the questions which continually crop up when the child comes to school; for he comes to school from his parents' home.

Now if the aim is to achieve an individual and harmonious relationship, the teacher is concerned with the welfare of the child possibly even more than the parents themselves to whom he looks for support. If he does not merely let the parents come and then proceed to give them information which they can make nothing much of, but if, after a parents' evening, he shows a further interest by visiting the parents in their home, then in receiving a child of school age, about 7 years old, into his class, he has taken on very much more than he thinks. He has the father, the mother and other people from the child's environment; they are standing shadowlike in the background. He has almost as much to do with them as with the child himself, especially where physiological-pathological matters are concerned. The teacher must take all this into account and work it out for himself; he must look at the situation as a whole in order really to understand the child, and above all to become clear in his own mind what he should do in regard to the child's environment. By building this bridge between himself and the parents, as he sees them in their home, a kind of support will be brought about, a support which is social in its nature and is at the same time both free and living.

To visit the parents in their home is necessary in order to foster in the parents a concern that nothing should occur which might damage the natural feeling a child must have for the authority of the teacher. A lot of work must be done between the college of teachers and the parent-body by means of an understanding imbued with feeling, with qualities of soul. Moreover the parent too, by getting to know the teachers, getting to know them pretty thoroughly, must break themselves of the tendency to be jealous of them, for indeed most parents are jealous of their children's teachers. They feel as if the teachers want to take the child away from them; but as soon as this feeling is present there is an end to what can be achieved educationally with the child. Such things, can, however, be put right if the teacher understands how to win the true support of the parents. This is what I wished to add to my previous remarks on the purpose of the teachers' conferences.

Now there is something else to be considered. We must learn to understand those moments in a child's life which are significant moments of transition. I have already referred to one such moment when the teaching, which up to this time has been imaginative and pictorial must pass over, for instance, into teaching the child about the nature of the plants. This point of time lies between the 9th and 10th year. It shows itself in the child as an inner restlessness; he asks all kinds of questions. What he asks has usually no great importance in so far as the content is concerned; but the fact that the questions are asked, that the child feels impelled to ask questions, this is undoubtedly of great significance.

The kind of relationship we establish with the child just at this time has great importance for the whole of his life. For what is it that indwells the soul of the child? It is something that can be observed in every child who is not pathological. Up to this age a child who has not been ruined by external influences accepts the authority of the teacher quite naturally; a healthy child who has not been ruined by being talked into all kinds of nonsensical ideas also has a healthy respect for every grown-up person. He looks up to such a person, taking him as an authority quite simply and as a matter of course. Just think back to your own childhood; realise what it means, particularly for the quite young child, to be able to say to himself; You may do what he does or what she does for they are good and worthy people. The child really requires nothing else than to place himself under an authority

In a certain sense this feeling is somewhat shaken between the 9th and 10th year; it is shaken simply in the course of the development of human nature itself. It is important to be able to perceive this clearly. At this time human nature experiences something quite special, which does not however rise up into the child's consciousness, but lives in indefinite sensations and feelings. The child is unable to give it expression, but it is there. What does the child now say to himself unconsciously? Earlier he said out of his instinctive feelings: If my teacher says something is good, then it is good; if he says something is bad, it is bad; if he says something is right, it is right; if he says it is wrong, it is wrong. If something gives my teacher pleasure and he says it pleases him, then it is beautiful; if he says something is ugly and it does not please him, then it is ugly. It is quite a matter of course for the young child to look upon his teacher as his model. But now, between the 9th and 10th year this inner certainty is somewhat shaken. The child begins to ask himself in his life of feeling : Where does he or she get it all from? Who is the teacher's authority? Where is this authority? At this moment the child begins to feel an inner urge to break through the visible human being, who until now has been for him a god, to that which stands behind him as supersensible or invisible God, or Divine Being. Now the teacher, facing the child, must contrive in some simple way to confirm this feeling in him. He must approach the child in such a way that he feels : Behind my teacher there is something supersensible which gives him support. He does not speak in an arbitrary way; he is a messenger from the Divine.

One must make the child aware of this. But how? Least of all by preaching. One can only give a hint in words, one will achieve nothing whatever by a pedantic approach. But if one comes up to the child and perhaps says something to him which as far as content goes has no special importance, if one says a few words which perhaps are quite unimportant but which are spoken in such a tone of voice that he sees : He or she has a heart, this heart itself believes in what is standing behind,—then something can be achieved. We must make the child aware of this standing within the universe, but we must make him aware of it in the right way. Even if he cannot yet take in abstract, rationalistic ideas, he already has enough understanding to come and ask a question : Oh, I would so much like to know . . . . Children of this age often come with such questions. If we now say to him : Just think, what I am able to give you I receive from the sun; if the sun were not there I should not be able to give you anything at all in life; if the divine power of the moon were not there to preserve for us while we sleep what we receive from the sun I should not be able to give you anything either. In so far as its content is concerned we have not said anything of particular importance. If however we say it with such warmth that the child perceives that we love the sun and the moon, then we can lead him beyond the stage at which he asks these questions and in the majority of cases this holds good for the whole of life. One must know that these critical moments occur in the child's life. Then quite of itself the feeling will arise : Up to this time when telling stories about the fir tree and the oak, about the buttercup and dandelion, or about the sunflower and the violet, I have spoken in fairytale fashion about Nature and in this way I have led the child into a spiritual world; but now the time has come when I can begin to tell stories taken from the Gospels. If we begin to do this earlier, or try to teach him anything in the nature of a catechism we destroy something in the child, but if we begin now, when he is trying to break through towards the spiritual world, we do something which the child demands with his whole being.

Now where is that book to be found in which the teacher can read what teaching is? The children themselves are this book. We should not learn to teach out of any other book than the one lying open before us and consisting of the children themselves; but in order to read in this book we need the widest possible interest in each individual child and nothing must divert us from this. Here the teacher may well experience difficulties and these must be consciously overcome.

Let us assume that the teacher has children of his own. In this case he is faced with a more direct and more difficult task than if he had no children. He must therefore be all the more conscious just in this respect and above all he must not hold the opinion that all children should be like his own. He must not think this even subconsciously. He must ask himself whether it is not the case that people who have children are subconsciously of the opinion that all children should be like theirs.

We see therefore that what the teacher has perforce to admit touches on the most intimate threads of the life of soul. And unless he penetrates to these intimate subconscious threads he will not find complete access to the children, while at the same time winning their full confidence. Children suffer great, nay untold damage if they come to believe that other children are the teacher's favourites. This must be avoided at all costs. It is, not so easily avoided as people usually think, but it can be avoided if the teacher is imbued with all those principles which can result from an anthroposophical knowledge of man. Then such a matter finds its own solution.

There is something which calls for special attention in con- nection with the theme I have chosen for this course of lectures, something which is connected with the significance of education for the whole world and for humanity. It lies in the very nature of human existence that the teacher, who has so much to do with children and who as a rule has so little opportunity of living outside his sphere of activity, needs some support from the outer world, needs necessarily to look out into this world. Why is it that teachers so easily become dried up? It happens because they have continually to stoop to the level of the child. We certainly have no reason to make fun of the teacher if, limited to the usual conceptual approach to teaching, he becomes dried up. We should nevertheless perceive where the danger lies, and the anthroposophical teacher is in a position to be specially aware of this. For if the average teacher's com- prehension of history gradually becomes that of a school text- book—and this may well happen in the course of a few years' teaching—where should he look for another kind of comprehen- sion, for ideas in keeping with what is truly human? How can the situation be amended? The time remaining to the teacher after his school week is usually spent trying to recover from fatigue, and often only parish pump politics plays a part in forming his attitude towards questions of world impor- tance. Thus the soul life of such a teacher does not turn outwards and enter into the kind of understanding which is necessary for a human being between say, the ages of 30 and 40. Furthermore he does not keep fit and well if he thinks that the best way to recuperate in leisure hours is to play cards or do something else which is in no way connected with the life of the spirit.

The situation of a teacher who is an anthroposophist, whose life is permeated with anthroposophy, is very different. His perspective of the world is continually widening; his sphere of

vision extends ever further and further. It is very easy to show
how these things affect each other—It is indicated by the fact
that the most enthusiastic anthroposophist, if, for instance, he
becomes a teacher of history, immediately tends to carry anthroposophy into his conception of history and so falls into the
error of wanting to teach not history, but anthroposophy. This
is also something one must try to avoid. It will be completely
avoided if such a teacher, having on the one hand his children
and on the other hand anthroposophy, feels the need of building a bridge between the school and the homes of the parents.
Even though anthroposophy is knowledge as applied to man,
understanding as applied to man, there are nevertheless neces-
sities in life which must be observed. How do people often think
today, influenced as they are by current ideas in regard to
educational reform or even by revolutionary ideas in this field?
I will not at this moment enter into what is said in socialist
circles, but will confine myself to what is thought by those
belonging to the prosperous middle classes. There the view is
held that people should get out of the town and settle in the
country in order that many children may be educated right
away from the town. Only so, it is felt, can they develop
naturally. And so on, and so on. But how does such a thought
fit into a more comprehensive conception of the world? It really
amounts to an admission of one's own helplessness. For the
point is not to think out some way in which a number of
children may be educated quite apart from the world, according to one's own intellectual, abstract ideas, but rather to
discover how children may be helped to grow into true human
beings within the social milieu which is their environment. One
must muster one's strength and not take children away from the
social milieu in which they are living. It is essential to have this
courage. It is something which is connected with the world
significance of education.

But then there must be a deep conviction that the world
must find its way into the school. The world must continue to
exist within the school, albeit in a childlike way. If therefore we
would stand on the ground of a healthy education we should

not think out all kinds of occupational activity intended only for children. For instance all kinds of things are devised for children to do. They must learn to plait; they must carry out all kinds of rather meaningless activities which have absolutely nothing to do with life, merely to keep them busy. Such methods can never serve any good purpose in the child's development. On the contrary, all play activity at school must be a direct imitation of life. Everything must proceed out of life, nothing should be thought out. Hence, in spite of the good intentions lying behind them, those things which have been introduced into the education of little children by Froebel or others are not directly related to the real development of the children. They are thought out, they belong to our rationalistic age. Nothing that is merely thought out should form part of a school's activity.

Above all there must be a secret feeling that life must hold sway everywhere in education. In this connection one can have quite remarkable experiences. I have told you already that the child who has reached the stage of changing his teeth should have the path of learning made smooth for him by means of painting or drawing. Writing—a form of drawing which has become abstract—should be developed out of a kind of painting-drawing or drawing-painting. But in doing this it should be borne in mind that the child is very sensitive to aesthetic impressions. A little artist is hidden somewhere inside him, and it is just here that quite interesting discoveries can be made. A really good teacher may be put in charge of a class, someone who is ready to carry out the things I have been explaining, someone who is full of enthusiasm and who says: One must simply do away with all the earlier methods of education and begin to educate in this new way! So now he starts off with this business of painting-drawing or drawing-painting. The pots of paint and the paint brushes are ready and the children take up their brushes. At this point one can have the following experience. The teacher simply has no idea of the difference between a colour that shines and one that does not shine. He has already become too old. In this respect one can have the strangest experiences. I once had the opportunity of telling an excellent chemist about our efforts to produce radiant, shining colours for the paintings in the Goetheanum and how we were experimenting with colours made out of plants. Thereupon he said: But today we are already able to do much better—today we actually have the means whereby we can produce colours which are irridescent and begin to shimmer when it is dark. This chemist understood not a word of what I had been saying; he immediately thought in terms of chemistry. Grown-up people often have no sense for a shining colour. Children still have this sense. Everything goes wonderfully with very few words if one is able to read out of the nature of childhood what the child still possesses. The teacher's guidance must however be understanding and artistic in its approach, then the child will find his way easily into everything his teacher wishes to bring to him.

All this can however only be brought about if we feel deeply that school is a place for young life; but at the same time we must realise what is suitable for adult life. Here we must cultivate a sensitivity as to what can and what cannot be done. Please let no one take offence at what I am about to say. Last year in the framework of a conference on anthroposophical education the following took place. There was the wish to show to a public audience what has such an important part to play in our education: Eurythmy. This was done, but it was done in the following manner. In this particular place children gave a demonstration of what they had learned at school in their eurythmy lessons and a performance showing eurythmy as an art was only given later. Things were not arranged so that first people were given the opportunity of gaining some understanding of eurythmy, so that they might perhaps say: Ah, so that is eurythmy, that is what has been introduced into the school. It was done the other way round; the children's eurythmy demonstration was given first place, with the result that the audience was quite unconvinced and had no idea what it was all about. Just imagine that up till now there had been no art of painting: then all of a sudden an exhibition was held showing how children begin to daub with colours! Just as little was it possible for those who were outside the anthroposophical movement to see in this children's demonstration what is really intended and what actually underlies anthroposophy and eurythmy. Such a demonstration only has meaning if eurythmy is first introduced as an art; for then people can see what part it has to play in life and its significance in the world of art. Then the importance of eurythmy in education will also be recognised. Otherwise people may well say : Today all kinds of whimsical ideas are rife in the world—and eurythmy will be looked upon as just such another whimsical idea.

These are things which must lead us, not only to prepare ourselves for our work in education in the old, narrow sense, but to work with a somewhat wider outlook so that the school is not sundered from life but is an inseparable part of it. This is just as important as to think out some extremely clever method in education. Again and again I have had to lay stress on the fact that it is the attitude of mind which counts, the attitude of mind and the gift of insight. It is obvious that not everything can be equally perfect; this goes without saying. I do beg you not to take amiss what I have just said; this applies also to anthroposophists. I appreciate everything that is done, as it is here, with such willing sacrifice. But if I were not to speak in this way the following might well happen. Because wherever there is light there are also strong shadows, so wherever efforts are made to do things in a more spiritual way, there too the darkest shadows arise. Here the danger is actually not less than in the usual conventional circles, but greater. And it is particularly necessary for us, if we are to be equal to the tasks with which we shall be faced in a life which is becoming more and more complicated, to be fully awake and aware of what life is demanding of human beings. Today we no longer have those sharply defined traditions which guided an earlier humanity. We can no longer content ourselves with what our forefathers deemed right; we must bring up our children so that they may be able to form their own judgments. It is therefore imperative to break through the narrow confines of our preconceived ideas and take our stand within the all-comprehensive life and work of the world. We must no longer, as in earlier times, continue to find simple concepts by means of which we would seek to explain far-reaching questions of life. For the most part, even if there is no desire to be pedantic, the attempt is made to characterise most things with superficial definitions, much in the same way as was done in a certain Greek school of philosophy. When the question was put : what is a man?—the explanation given was as follows : A man is a living being who stands on two legs and has no feathers.—Many definitions which are given today are based on the same pattern,—But the next day, after someone had done some hard thinking as to what might lie behind these portentous words, he brought with him a plucked goose, for this was a being able to stand on two legs and having no feathers and he now asserted that this was a man. This is only an extreme case of what you find for instance in Goethe's play, "Goetz von Berlechingen," where the little boy begins to relate what he knows about geography. When he comes to his own district he describes it according to his lesson book and then goes on to describe a man whose development has taken place in this same neighbourhood. He has however not the faintest idea that the latter is his father. Out of sheer "erudition", based on what he has learned out of the book, he does not know his own father. Nevertheless these things do not go so far as the experience I once had in Weimar, where there are, of course, newspapers. These are produced in the way that usually happens in small places. Bits and pieces of news regarded as suitable are cut out of newspapers belonging to larger towns and inserted into the paper in question. So on one occasion, on 22nd January, we in Weimar read the following item of news : Yesterday a violent thunderstorm broke over our town. This piece of news had, however, been taken out of the *Leipziger Nachrichten*.

Similar things happen in life and we are continually caught in the web of their confusion. People theorise in abstract concepts. They study the theory of relativity and in so doing get the notion that it is all the same whether someone travels by car to Osterbeek or whether Osterbeek comes to him. If however anyone should wish to draw a conclusion based on reality he would have to say : If the car is not used it does not suffer wear and tear and the chauffeur does not get tired. Should the opposite be the case the resulting effect will likewise be opposite. If one thinks in this way then, without drawing a comparison between every line and movement, he will know out of an inner commonsense that his own being is changed when from a state of rest it is brought into movement. Bearing in mind the kind of thinking prevalent today, it is no wonder that a theory of relativity develops out of it when attention is turned to things in isolation. If however one goes back to reality it will become apparent that there is no accord between reality and what is thought out on the basis of mere relationship. Today, whether or not we are learned or clever we live perpetually outside reality; we live in a world of ideas in much the same way as the little boy in *Goetz von Berlichingen*, who did not know his father, in spite of having read a description of him in his geography book. We do not live in such a way as to have direct contact with reality.

But this is what we must bring into the school; we must face this direct impact of reality. We are able to do so if above all we learn to understand the true nature of man and what is intimately connected with him. It is for this reason that again and again I have to point out how easy it is for people today to assert that the child should be taught pictorially, by means of object lessons, and that nothing should be brought to him that is beyond his immediate power of comprehension. But in so doing we are drawn into really frightful trivialities. I have already mentioned the calculating machine. Now just consider the following : At the age of 8 I take something in but I do not really understand it. All I know is that it is my teacher who says it. Now I love my teacher. He is quite naturally my authority. Because he has said it I accept it with my whole heart. At the age of 15 I still do not understand it. But when I am 35 I meet with an experience in life which calls up, as though from wonderful spiritual depths, what I did not understand when I was 8 years old, but which I accepted solely on the authority of the teacher whom I loved. Because *he* was my authority I felt sure it must be true. Now life brings me another experience and suddenly, in a flash, I understand the earlier one. All this time it had remained hidden within me, and now life grants me the possibility of understanding it. Such an experience gives rise to a tremendous sense of obligation. And one cannot do otherwise than say: Sad indeed it is for anyone who experiences no moments in life when out of his own inner being something rises up into consciousness which he accepted long ago on the basis of authority and which he is only now able to understand. No one should be deprived of such an experience, for in later years it is the source of enthusiastic and purposeful activity in life.*

But let us add something else. I said that between the change of teeth and puberty children should not be given moral precepts, but in the place of these care should be taken to ensure that what is good pleases them because it pleases their teacher, and what is bad displeases them because it displeases their teacher. During the second period of life everything should be built up on sympathy with the good, antipathy for the bad. Then moral feelings are implanted deeply in the soul and there is established a sense of moral well-being in experiencing what is good and a sense of moral discomfort in experiencing what is bad. Now comes the time of puberty. Just as walking is fully developed during the first 7 years, speech during the second 7 years, so during the third 7 years of life thinking comes fully into its own. It becomes independent. This only takes place with the oncoming of puberty; only then are we really capable of forming a judgment . If at this time, when we begin to form thoughts out of an inner urge, feelings have already been implanted in us in the way I have indicated, then a good foundation has been laid and we are able to form judgments. For instance: this pleases me and I am in duty bound to act in accordance with it; that displeases me and it is my duty to leave it alone. The significance of this is that duty itself grows out of pleasure and displeasure; it is not instilled into me, but

* Walter de la Mare has described this experience and the joy of saying: "Ah, so that was the meaning of that."

grows out of pleasure and displeasure. This is the awakening of true freedom in the human soul. We experience freedom through the fact that the sense for what is moral is the deepest individual impulse of the individual human soul. If a child has been led to a sense of the moral by an authority which is self-understood, so that the moral lives for him in the world of feeling, then after puberty the conception of duty works out of his individual inner human being. This is a healthy procedure. In this way we lead the children rightly to the point at which they are able to experience what individual freedom is. Why do people not have this experience today? They do not have it because they cannot have it, because before puberty a knowledge of good and bad was instilled into them; what they should and should not do was inculcated. But moral instruction which pays no heed to a right approach by gradual stages dries up the human being, makes out of him, as it were, a skeleton of moral precepts on which the conduct of life is hung like clothes on a coathanger.

If everything in life is to form a harmonious whole, education must follow a quite different course from the one usually pursued. It must be understood that the child goes through one stage between birth and the change of teeth, another between the change of teeth and puberty and yet another between puberty and the age of 21. Why does the child do this or that in the years before he is 7? Because he wants to imitate. He wants to do what he sees being done in his immediate surroundings. But what he does must be connected with life, it must be led over into living activity. We can do very much to help bring this about if we accustom the child to feel gratitude for what he receives from his environment. Gratitude is the basic virtue in the child between birth and the change of teeth. If he sees that everyone who stands in some kind of relationship to him in the outer world shows gratitude for what he receives from this world; if, in confronting the outer world and wanting to imitate it, the child sees the kind of gestures that express gratitude, then a great deal is done towards establishing in him the right moral human attitude. Gratitude is what belongs to the first 7 years of life.

If gratitude has been developed in the child during this first period it will now be easy between the 7th and 14th years to develop what must be the activating impulse in everything he does. This is love. Love is the virtue belonging to the second period of life. And only after puberty does there develop out of what has been experienced with love between the change of teeth and puberty that most inward of human impulses, the impulse of duty. Then what Goethe once expressed so beautifully becomes the guiding line for life. Goethe asks: "What is duty? It is when one loves what one commands oneself." This is the goal to which we must attain. We shall however only reach it when we are led to it by stages: Gratitude— Love—Duty.

A few days ago we saw how things arising out of an earlier epoch of life are carried over into later ones. I spoke about this in answer to a question. Now I must point out that this has its good side also; it is something that must be. Of course I do not mean that gratitude should cease with the 7th year or love with the 14th year. But here we have the very secret of life: what is developed in one epoch can be carried over into later epochs, but there will be metamorphosis, intensification, change. We should not be able to carry over the good belonging to one epoch were there not also the possibility of carrying over the bad. Education however must concern itself with this and see to it that the force inherent in the human being, enabling him to carry over something out of an earlier into a later epoch, is used to further what is good. In order to achieve this however we must make use of what I said yesterday. Let us take the case of a child in whom, owing to certain underlying pathological tendencies, there is the possibility of moral weakness in later life. We perceive that what is good does not really please him, neither does what is bad awaken his displeasure. In this respect he makes no progress. Then, because love is not able to develop in the right way between the 7th and the 14th year, we try to make use of

what is inherent in human nature itself, we try to develop in
the child a real sense of gratitude, to educate him so that he
turns with real gratitude to the self-understood authority of the
teacher. If we do this, things will improve in respect of love
also. A knowledge of human nature will prevent us from
setting about things in such a way that we say : This child is
lacking in love for the good and antipathy for the bad; I must
instil this into him ! It cannot be done. But things will go of
themselves if we foster gratitude in the child. It is therefore
essential to know the part gratitude plays in relation to love
in the course of moral development in life; we must know that
gratitude is a natural development in human nature during
the first years of life and that love is active in the whole
human organisation as a quality of soul before it comes to
physical expression at puberty. For what then makes itself felt
outwardly is active between the years of 7 and 14 as the
deepest principle of life and growth in man; it weaves and
lives in his inmost being. Here, where it is possible to discuss
these things on a fundamental basis, I may be allowed to say
what is undoubtedly a fact. When a teacher has once understood the nature of an education that takes its stand on a real
knowledge of man, when on the one side he is engaged on the
actual practice of such an education, and when on the other
side he is actively concerned in the study of the anthroposophical conception of the world, then each works reciprocally
on the other. For the teacher must work in the school in such
a way that he takes as a foregone conclusion the fact that
love is inwardly active in the child and then comes to outer
expression in sexuality.

The anthroposophical teacher also attends meetings where
the world conception of anthroposophy is studied. There he
hears from those who have already acquired the necessary knowledge derived from Initiation Wisdom about such things as the
following : The human being consists of physical body, etheric
body, astral body and ego. Between the 7th and 14th years the
etheric body works mainly on the physical body; the astral body
descends into the physical and etheric bodies at the time of

puberty. But anyone able to penetrate deeply into these matters, anyone able to perceive more than just physical processes, whose perceptions always include spiritual processes and, when the two are separated, can perceive each separately, such a man or woman can discern how in an 11 or 12 year old boy the astral body is already sounding, chiming, as it were, with the deeper tone which will first make itself heard outwardly at puberty. And a similar process takes place in the astral body of an 11 or 12 year old girl.

These things are actual, and if they are regarded as realities they will throw light on life's problems. It is just concerning these very things that one can have quite remarkable experiences. I will not withhold such experiences. In the year 1906 I gave a number of lectures in Paris before a relatively small circle of people. I had prepared my lectures bearing these people specially in mind, taking account of the fact that in this circle there were men of letters, writers, artists and others who at this particular epoch were concerned with quite specific questions. Since then things have changed, but at that time a certain something lay behind the questions in which these people were interested. They were of the type which gets up in the morning filled with the notion : I belong to a Society which is interested in the history of literature, the history of the arts; when one belongs to such a Society one wears this sort of tie, and since the year so-and-so one no longer goes to parties in tails or dinner jacket. One is aware of this when invited to dine where these and similar topics are discussed. Then in the evening one goes to the theatre and sees plays which deal with current problems ! The so-called poets then write such plays themselves. At first there is a man of deep and inward sensibility, out of whose heart these great problems arise in an upright and honourable way. First there is a Strindberg. Later on follow those who popularise Strindberg for a wider public. And so, at the time I held these Paris lectures, that particular problem was much discussed which shortly before had driven the tragic Weininger to suicide. The problem which Weininger portrays in so childlike yet noble a fashion in *Geschlecht und*

Charakter (Sex and Character) was the problem of the day. After I had dealt with those things which were essential to an understanding of the subject I proceeded to explain that every human being has one sex in the external physical body, but bears the other sex in the etheric body. So that the woman is man in etheric body, and the man is woman. Every human being in his totality is bi-sexual; he bears the other sex within him. I can actually observe when something of this kind is said, how people begin to look out of their astral bodies, how they suddenly feel that a problem is solved for them over which they have chewed for a long time, and how a certain restlessness, but a pleasant kind of restlessness is perceptible among the audience. Where there are big problems, not merely insignificant sensations in life, but where there is real enthusiasm, even if it is sometimes close to small talk, then again one becomes aware of how a sense of relief, of being freed from a burden, emanates from those present.

So the anthroposophical teacher always looks on big problems as being something which can work on him in such a way that he remains *human* at every age of life; so that he does not become dried up, but remains fresh and alert and able to bring this freshness with him into the school. It is a completely different thing whether a teacher only looks into text books and imparts their content to the children, or whether he steps out of all this and, as human being pure and simple, confronts the great perspectives of the world. In this case he carries what he himself has absorbed into the atmosphere of the classroom when he enters it and gives his lesson.

LECTURE VII

Arnheim, 23rd July, 1924

From the lectures which have been given here, dealing with an art of education built upon the foundation of a knowledge of man, you formed a clear idea of what should be the relation between teacher and taught. What lives in the soul, in the whole personality of the teacher, works in hundreds of unseen ways from the educator over to the children his pupils. But it only works if the educator bears within his soul a true and penetrating knowledge of man, a knowledge which is approaching the transition leading over into spiritual experience. And today I must precede my lecture with a few remarks which may serve to clarify what is to be understood in the anthroposophical sense by spiritual experience, for just in regard to this the most erroneous ideas abound.

It is so easy to think that in the first place spiritual perception must rise above everything of a material nature. Certainly one can attain to a deeply satisfying soul experience, even though this may be coloured by egotistical feeling, when, rising above the material, one ascends into the spiritual world. We must do this also. For we can only learn to know the spiritual when we acquire this knowledge in the realm of the spirit; and anthroposophy must deal in many ways with spiritual realms and spiritual beings which have nothing to do with the physical world of the senses. And when it is a question of learning to know what is so necessary for modern man, to know about the life between death and a new birth, the actual supersensible life of man before birth or conception and the life after death, then we must certainly rise up to body-free, supersensible, super-physical perception. But we must of course act and work within the physical world; we must stand firmly in this world. If we are teachers, for instance, we are not called upon to teach disembodied souls. We cannot ask ourselves, if we wish to be teachers; What is our relationship to souls who have passed through death and are living in the spiritual world?—But if we wish to work as teachers between birth and death, we must ask ourselves : In what way does a soul dwell within the physical body? And indeed we must consider this, at any rate for the years after birth. It is actually a question of being able to gaze with the spirit into the material. And Anthroposophy, Spiritual Science, is in this respect largely a matter of looking into the material with the spirit.

But the opposite procedure is also right : one must penetrate with spiritual vision into the spiritual world, penetrate so far that the spiritual seems to be every bit as full of "living sap" as anything in the sense world; one must be able to speak about the spiritual as if it radiated colours, as if its tones were audible, as if it were standing before one as much "embodied" as the beings of the sense world. In anthroposophy it is first this which causes abstract philosophers such intense annoyance. They find it exceedingly annoying that the spiritual investigator describes the spiritual world and spiritual beings in such a way that it seems as if he might meet these beings at any moment, just as he might meet human beings; that he might hold out his hand to them and speak with them. He describes these spiritual beings just as though they were earthly beings; indeed his description makes them appear almost as if they were earthly beings. In other words, he portrays the spiritual in pictures comprehensible to the senses. He does this in full consciousness, because for him the spiritual is an absolute reality. There is some truth in it, too, because a real knowledge of the whole world leads to the point at which one can "give one's hand" to spiritual beings, one can meet them and converse with them. That strikes the philosopher, who is only willing to conceive the spiritual world by means of abstract concepts, as being paradoxical, to say the least of it; nevertheless such a description is necessary. On the other hand it is also necessary to look right through a human being, so that the material part of him vanishes completely, and he stands there purely as a spirit. When however a non-anthroposophist wishes to look upon a man as spirit, then this man is not only a ghost, but something much less than a ghost. He is a sort of coat-hanger on which are hung all kinds of concepts which serve to activate mental pictures and so on. In comparison a ghost is quite respectably solid, but a human being as described by such a philosopher is really indecently naked in regard to the spirit. In anthroposophy physical man is contemplated by means of purely spiritual perception, but nevertheless he still has brains, liver, lungs and so on; he is a concrete human being; he has everything that is found in him when the corpse is dissected. Everything that is spiritual in its nature works right down into the physical. The physical is observed spiritually, but nevertheless man possesses a physical body. He can even "blow his nose" in a spiritual sense; spiritual reality goes as far as this. Only by becoming aware that in contemplating the physical it can become completely spiritual, and in contemplating the spiritual it can be brought down again so that it becomes almost physical, only by this awareness can the two be brought together. The physical human being can be contemplated in a condition of health and illness; but the ponderable material vanishes, it becomes spiritual. And the spiritual can be contemplated as it is between death and a new birth and, pictorially speaking, it becomes physical. Thus the two are brought together.

Man learns to penetrate into the real human being through the fact that there are these two possibilities, the possibility of beholding the spiritual by means of sense-perceptible pictures and the possibility of beholding spiritual entities in the world of the senses. If therefore the question arises : How may spiritual vision be understood in its real and true sense?—the answer must be : One must learn to see all that appertains to the senses in a spiritual way, and one must look at the spiritual in a way that is akin to the senses. This seems paradoxical, but it is so. And only after entering into what I have just said and realising its truth, can one reach the point of looking at the child in the right way.

I will give you an example. A child in my class becomes paler and paler. I see this increasing pallor. It shows itself in the physical life of the child, but we gain nothing by going to the doctor and getting him to prescribe something that will bring back the child's colour; for, should we do so, the following may well be the result : The child grows pale and this is observed, so the school doctor comes and prescribes something which is intended to restore the lost colour. Now even if the doctor has acted perfectly correctly and has prescribed a quite good remedy, which he must do in such cases, nevertheless something rather strange will be observed in the child who is now "cured". Indeed in a sense he is cured, and anyone in a position of seniority to the doctor, who might be called upon to write a testimonial for the authorities, could well say that the doctor had cured the child—later, however, it is noticeable at school that the child who has been cured in this way is no longer able to take things in properly; he has become fidgety and restless and has lost all power of attention. Whereas previously he used to sit in his place, pale and somewhat indolent, he now begins to pommel his neighbour; and whereas previously he had dipped his pen gently into the inkwell, he now sticks it in with so much force that the ink spurts up and bespatters his exercise book. The doctor did his duty but the result was the reverse of beneficial, for it sometimes happens that people who have been "cured" suffer later on from extraordinary after-effects.

Again, in such a case it is important to recognise what actually lies at the root of the trouble. If the teacher is able to penetrate into the soul-spiritual cause of what finds its outer physical expression in a growing pallor, he will become aware of the following. The power of memory which works in the soul-spiritual is nothing else than the transformed, metamorphosed force of growth; and to develop the forces of growth and nourishment is just the same, albeit on a different level, as it is, on a higher level, to cultivate the memory, the power of recollection. It is the same force, but in a different stage of metamorphosis. Pictured systematically we can say : During the first years of a child's life both these forces are merged into one another, they have not yet separated; later on memory separates from this state of fusion and becomes a power in itself, and the same holds good for the power of growth and nourishment. The small child still needs the forces which later develop memory in order that he may digest milk and the stomach be able to carry out its functions; this is why he cannot remember anything. Later, when the power of memory is no longer the servant of the stomach, when the stomach makes fewer demands on it and only retains a minimum of these forces, then part of the forces of growth are transformed into a quality of soul, into memory, the power of recollection. Possibly the other children in the class are more robust, the division between the power of memory and of growth may be better balanced, and so, perhaps, the teacher pays less heed to a child who in this respect has little to fall back on. If this is the case it may easily happen that his power of memory is overburdened, too much being demanded of this emancipated faculty. The child grows pale and the teacher must needs say to himself : "I have put too much strain on your memory; that is why you have grown so pale." It is very noticeable that when such a child is relieved of this burden he gets his colour back again. But the teacher must understand that the growing pale is connected with what he has done himself in the first place, by overburdening the child with what has to be remembered. It is very important to be able to look right into physical symptoms and to realise that if a child grows too pale it is because his memory has been overburdened.

But I may have another child in the class who from time to time becomes strikingly red in the face and this also may be a cause for concern. If this occurs, if a hectic red flush makes its appearance, it is very easy to recognise certain accompanying conditions in the child's soul-life; for in the strangest way, at times when one would least expect it, such children fall into a passion of anger, they become over-emotional. Naturally there can be the same procedure as before : A rush of blood to the head—something must be prescribed for it. Of course, in such cases too, the doctor does his duty. But it is important to know something else, namely, that this child, in contrast to the other, has been neglected in respect of his faculty of memory. Too many of these forces have gone down into the forces of his growth and nourishment. In this case one must try to make greater demands on the child's power of memory. If this is done such symptoms will disappear.

Only when we take into our ken the physical and the spiritual as united do we learn to recognise many things in the school which are in need of readjustment. We train ourselves to recognise this interconnection of physical and spiritual when we look at what lies between them as part of the whole human organisation, namely, the temperaments. The children come to school and they have the four temperaments, varied of course with all kinds of transitions and mixtures: the melancholic, the phlegmatic, the sanguine and the choleric. In our Waldorf education great value is laid on being able to enter into and understand the child according to his temperament. The actual seating of the children in the classroom is arranged on this basis. We try for instance to discover which are the choleric children; these we place together, so that it is possible for the teacher to know : There in that corner I have the children who tend to be choleric. In another, the phlegmatic children are seated, somewhere in the middle are the sanguines and again somewhere else, grouped together are the melancholics. This method of grouping has great advantages. Experience shows that after a while the phlegmatics become so bored with sitting together that, as a means of getting rid of this boredom, they begin to rub it off on one another. On the other hand the cholerics pommel one another so much that quite soon this too becomes very much better. It is the same with the fidgety ways of the sanguines, and the melancholics also see what it is like when others are absorbed in melancholy. Thus to handle the children in such a way that one sees how "like reacts favourably on like" is very good even from an external point of view, quite apart from the fact that by doing so the teacher has the possibility of surveying the whole class, for this is much easier when children of similar temperament are seated together.

Now however we come to the essential point. The teacher must enter so deeply into the nature of the human being that he is able to deal in a truly practical way with the choleric, the sanguine, the melancholic temperament. There will naturally be cases where it is necessary to build the bridge of which I have already spoken, the bridge between school and home, and this must be done in a friendly and tactful way. Let us suppose that I have a melancholic child in the class, with whom I can do scarcely anything. I am unable to enter into his difficulties in the right way. He broods and is withdrawn, is occupied with himself and pays no heed to what is going on in the class. If one applies an education that is not founded on a knowledge of man one may think that everything possible should be done to attract his attention and draw him out of himself. As a rule however such a procedure will make things still worse; the child broods more than ever. All these means of effecting a cure, thought out in such an amateurish way, help but little. What helps most in such a case is the spontaneous love which the teacher feels for the child, for then he is aware of sympathy, and this stirs and moves what is more subconscious in him. We may be sure that anything in the way of exhortation is not only wasted effort, but is actually harmful, for the child becomes more melancholic than before. But in class it helps greatly if one tries to enter into the melancholy, tries to discover the direction to which it tends, and then shows interest in the child's attitude of mind, becoming in a certain way, by what one does oneself, melancholic with the melancholic child. As a teacher one must bear within oneself all four temperaments in harmonious, balanced activity. And this balance, which is in direct contradiction to the child's melancholy, if it is continued and is always present in one's relationship to the child, is perceived by him. He sees what kind of man his teacher is by what underlies his words. And in this way, creeping in behind the mask of melancholy, which the teacher accepts, there is implanted in the child his teacher's loving sympathy. This can be of great help in the class.

But now we will go further, for we must know that every

manifestation of melancholy in a human being is connected with some irregularity in the function of the liver. This may seem unlikely to the physicist, but it is nevertheless a fact that every kind of melancholy, especially if it goes so far in a child as to become pathological, is due to some irregularity of this kind. In such a case I shall turn to the parents of the child and say : "It would be good to put more sugar in his food than you usually do." He needs sweet things, for sugar helps to normalise the function of the liver. And by giving the mother this advice : "Give the child more sugar"—I shall get school and home working together, in order to lift this melancholy out of the pathological condition into which it has sunk and so create the possibility of finding the right constitutional treatment.

Or I may have a sanguine child, a child who goes from one impression to another; who always wants what comes next, almost before he has got hold of what precedes it; who makes a strong start, showing great interest in everything, but whose interest soon fades out. He is not dark as a rule, but fair. I am now faced with the problem of how to deal with him at school. In everything I do I shall try to be more sanguine than the child. I shall change the impressions I make on him extremely quickly, so that he is not left hurrying from one impression to another at his own sweet will, but must come with me at my pace. This is quite another story. He soon has enough of it and finally gives up. But between what I myself do in bringing impressions to the child in this very sanguine way, and what he does himself in hurrying from one thing to another in accordance with his temperament, there is gradually established in him, as a kind of natural reaction, a more harmonious condition. So I can treat the child in this way. I can present him with rapidly changing impressions, always thinking out something new, so that he sees, as it were, first black, then white, and must continually hurry from one thing to another. I now get in touch with the mother and I will certainly hear from her that the child has an inordinate love of sugar. Perhaps he is given a great many sweets or somehow manages to get hold of them, or maybe the family as such is very fond of sweet dishes.

If this is not so, then his mother's milk was too sweet, it contained too much sugar. So I explain this to the mother and advise her to put the child on a diet for a time and reduce the amount of sugar she gives him. In this way, by arranging with the parents for a diet with little sugar, co-operation is brought about between home and school. The reduction of sugar will gradually help to overcome the abnormality which, in the case of this child also, is caused by irregularity in the activity of the liver in respect of the secretion of gall. There is a very slight, barely noticeable irregularity in the secretion of gall. Here too I shall recognise the help given me by the parents.

So we must know as a matter of actual fact where, so to speak, the physical stands within the spiritual, where it is one with the Spiritual.

It is possible to go into more detail and say : A child shows a rapid power of comprehension, he understands everything very easily; but when after a few days I come back to what he grasped so quickly and about which I was so pleased, it has vanished; it is no longer there. Here again I can do a good deal at school to improve matters. I shall try to put forward and explain something which demands a more concentrated attention than the child is accustomed to give. He understands things too quickly, it is not necessary for him to make enough inner effort, so that what he learns may really impress itself on him. I shall therefore give him hard nuts to crack, I shall give him something which is more difficult to grasp and demands more attention. This I can do at school. But now once more I get in touch with the child's parents and from them I may hear various things. What I am now saying will not hold good in every case, but I want to give some indication of the path to be pursued. I shall have a tactful discussion with the mother, avoiding any suspicion of riding the high horse by talking down to her and giving her instructions. From our conversation I shall find out how she caters for the family and I shall most likely discover that this particular child eats too many potatoes. The situation is a little difficult because now the mother may say, "Well, you tell me that my child eats too many potatoes;

but my neighbour's little daughter eats more still and she has not the same failing, so the trouble cannot be caused by potato-eating." Something of this kind is what the mother may say. And nevertheless it does come from eating potatoes, because the organisation of children differs, one child being able to assimilate more potato and another less. And the curious thing is this. The condition of a particular child shows that he has been getting too many potatoes; it is shown by the fact that his memory does not function as it should. Now in this case the remedy is not to be found by giving him fewer potatoes. It may even happen that this is done and there is some improvement; but after a time things are no better than before. Here the immediate reduction of the amount of potato does not bring about the required effect, but it is a question of gradually breaking a habit, of exercising the activity needed in order to break a habit. So one must say to the mother, "For the first week give the child a tiny bit less potato; for the second week a very little less still; and continue in this way, so that the child is actively engaged in accustoming himself to eating only a small amount of potato. In this case it is a question of breaking a habit, and here one will see what a healing effect can be induced just by this means.

Now idealists, so-called, very likely reproach anthroposophy and maintain that it is materialistic. They actually do so. When for example an anthroposophist says that a child who comprehends easily but does not retain what he has learnt, should have his potato ration gradually decreased, then people say : You are an absolute materialist. Nevertheless there exists such an intimate interplay between matter and spirit that one can only work effectively when one can penetrate matter with spiritual perception and master it through spiritual knowledge. It is hardly necessary to say how greatly these things are sinned against in our present-day social life. But if a teacher is open to a world conception which reveals wide vistas he will arrive at an understanding of these things. He must only extend his outlook. For instance it will impress a teacher favourably and help him to gain an understanding of children if he learns how little sugar is consumed in Russia and how much in England. And if he proceeds to compare the Russian with the English temperament he will readily understand what an effect sugar has on temperament. It is advantageous to learn to know the world, so that this knowledge can come to our assistance in the tasks of every day. But now I will add something else. In Baden, in Germany, there is a remarkable monument erected as a memorial to Drake. I once wanted to know what was specially significant about this Drake, so I looked it up in an encyclopaedia and read : In Offenburg a monument was erected in memory of Drake because he was thought, albeit erroneously, to be the man who introduced the potato into Europe. There it stands in black and white. So a memorial was erected in honour of this man because he was considered to be the one who introduced the potato into Europe. He didn't do so, but nevertheless he has got a memorial in Offenburg.

The potato was, however, intoduced into Europe in comparatively recent times. And now I am going to tell you something about which you can laugh as much as you like. Nevertheless it is the truth. It is possible to study how the faculties of intelligence in human beings are related in their development from the time when there were no potatoes to the time when they were introduced. And, as you know, the potato is made use of in alcohol-distilleries. So potatoes suddenly began to play an important part in the development of European humanity. If you compare the increasing use of the potato with the curve of the development of intelligence, you will find that in comparison with the present day people living in the pre-potato age grasped things with less detail, but what they grasped they held fast. Their nature tended to be conservative, it was deeply inward. After the introduction of the potato people became quicker in regard to intelligent mobility of comprehension, but what they took in was not retained, it did not sink in deeply. The history of the development of the intelligence runs parallel with that of potato-eating. So here again we have an example of how anthroposophy explains this materialistically. But so it is. And much might be learned about cultural history if people everywhere could only know how in man's subconsciousness the external physical seizes hold of the spiritual. This becomes apparent in the nature of his desires.

Let us now choose as an example someone who has to write a great deal. Every day he has to write articles for the newspapers, so that he is obliged "to chew his pen" in order to produce what is necessary. If one has been through this oneself one can talk about it, but one has no right just to criticise others unless one speaks out of personal experience. While cogitating and biting one's pen one feels the need of coffee, for drinking coffee helps cohesion of thought. Thoughts become more logical when one drinks coffee than if one refrains from doing so. A journalist must needs enjoy coffee, for if he does not drink it his work takes more out of him. Now, as a contrast, let us take a diplomat. Call to mind what a diplomat had to acquire before the world war. He had to learn to use his legs in a special, approved manner; in the social circles in which he moved he had to learn to glide rather than set his foot down firmly as plainer folk do. He had also to be able to have thoughts which are somewhat fleeting and fluid. If a diplomat has a logical mind he will quite certainly fail in his profession and be unsuccessful in his efforts to help the nations solve their dilemmas. When diplomats are together— well, then one does not say they are having their coffee but they are having tea— for at such times there is the need to drink one cup of tea after another, so that the interchange of thought does not proceed in logical sequence, but springs as far as possible from one idea to the next. This is why diplomats love to drink tea; tea releases one thought from the next, it makes thinking fluid and fleeting, it destroys logic. So we may say : Writers are lovers of coffee, diplomats lovers of tea, in both cases out of a perfectly right instinct.

If we know this, we shall not look upon it as an infringement of human freedom. For obviously logic is not a product of coffee, it is only an unconscious, subconscious help towards it. The soul therefore remains free.

It is just when we are bearing the child especially in mind that it is necessary to look into relationships such as these, about which we get some idea when we can say : Tea is the drink for diplomats, coffee the drink for writers, and so on. Then we are also able gradually to gain an insight into the effects produced by the potato. The potato makes great demands on the digestion; moreover very small, almost homeopathic doses come from the digestive organs and rise up into the brain. This homeopathic dose is nevertheless very potent, it stimulates the forces of abstract intelligence. At this point I may perhaps be allowed to divulge something further. If we examine the substance of the potato through the microscope we obtain the well-known form of carbohydrates, and if we observe the astral body of someone who has eaten a large portion of potatoes we notice that in the region of the brain, about 3 centimetres behind the forehead, the potato substance begins to be active here also and to form the same eccentric circles. The movements of the astral body take on a similarity with the substance of the potato and the potato-eater becomes exceptionally intelligent. He bubbles over with intelligence, but this does not last, it is quite transient. Must one then not admit, provided one concedes that man possesses spirit and soul, that it is not altogether foolish and fantastic to speak of the spirit and to speak of it in images taken from the world of sense? Those who want always to speak of the spirit in abstract terms present us with nothing of a truly spiritual nature. It is otherwise with those who are able to bring the spirit down to earth in sense-perceptible pictures. Such a man can say that in the case of someone bubbling over with intelligence potato-substance takes on form in the brain, but does so in the spiritual sense. In this way we learn to recognise subtle and delicate differentiations and transitions. We discover that tea as regards its effects on logic makes a cleavage between thoughts, but it does not stimulate thinking. In saying that diplomats have a predilection for tea one does not imply that they can produce thoughts. On the other hand potatoes do stimulate thoughts. Swift as lightning they shoot thoughts upwards, only to let them vanish away again. But, accompanying this swift upsurging of thoughts, which can also take place in children, there goes a parallel process, an undermining of the digestive system. We shall be able to see in children whose digestive system is upset in this way, so that they complain of constipation, that all kinds of useless yet clever thoughts shoot up into their heads, thoughts which they certainly lose again but which nevertheless have been there.

I mention these things in detail so that you may see how the soul-spiritual and the physical must be looked upon as a whole, as a unity, and how in the course of human development a state of things must again be brought about which is able to hold together the most varied streams of culture. At the present time we are living in an epoch in which they are completely sundered from one another. This becomes clear to us however when we are able to look somewhat more deeply into the history of the evolution of mankind.

Today we separate religion, art and science from one another. And the guardians of religion, do all in their power to preserve religion from being encroached upon in any way by science. They maintain that religion is a matter of faith, and science belongs elsewhere. Science has its base where nothing is based on faith, where everything is founded on knowledge. But if one is to succeed in separating them in this way, the spiritual is cut off from science and the world is cut off from religion, with the result that religion becomes abstract and science devoid of spirit. Art is completely emancipated. In our time there are people, who, when one would like to tell them something about the supersensible, assume an air of clever superiority and regard one as superstitious: "Poor fellow! We know all that is sheer nonsense!"—But then a Bjornsen or someone else writes something or other in which such things play a part; something of the kind is introduced into art and thereupon everybody runs after it and enjoys in art what was rejected in the form of knowledge. Superstition sometimes appears in strange guise. I once had an acquaintance—such actual examples should most certainly be brought into the art of education, an art which can only be learned from life—I once had an acquaintance who was a dramatist. On one occasion I met him in the street; he was running extraordinarily quickly, perspiring as he went. It was 3 minutes to 8 o'clock in the evening. I asked him where he was going at such a pace. He was, however, in a great hurry and only said that he must rush to catch the post, for the post office closed at 8 o'clock. I did not detain him, but psychologically I was interested to know the reason for his haste so I waited until he returned. He came back after a while in a great heat, and then he was more communicative. I wanted to know why he was in such a hurry to catch the post, and he said, "Oh, I have just sent off my play." Previously he had always said that this play was not yet finished, and he said the same again now; "It is true that it is still unfinished, but I wanted particularly to get it off today, so that the director may receive it tomorrow. I have just written him a letter to this effect asking him to let me have it back. For you see, if a play is sent off before the end of the month it may be chosen for a performance; there is no chance otherwise!"—Now this dramatist was an extremely enlightened, intelligent man. Nevertheless he believed that if a play was despatched on a definite day it would be accepted, even if, owing to being unfinished, it had to be returned. From this incident you can see how things which people are apt to despise creep into some hole and corner, out of which they raise their heads at the very next opportunity.

This is especially the case with a child. We believe we have managed to rid him of something, but straightaway there it is again somewhere else. We must learn to look out for this. We must open our hearts when making a study of man, so that a true art of education may be based on an understanding and knowledge of the human being. Only by going into details shall we be able to fathom all these things.

Today then, as I was saying, religion, art and science are spoken about as though they were entirely unrelated. This was not so in long past ages of human evolution. Then they were a complete unity. At that time there existed Mystery Centres which were also centres for education and culture, centres dedicated at one and the same time to the cultivation of religion, art and science. For then what was imparted as knowledge consisted of pictures, representations and mental images of the spiritual world. These were received in such an intuitive and comprehensive way that they were transformed into external sense-perceptible symbols and thereby became the basis of cultic ceremonial. Science was embodied in such cults, as was art also; for what was taken from the sphere of knowledge and given external form must perforce be beautiful. Thus in those times a divine truth, a moral goodness and a sense-perceptible beauty existed in the Mystery Centres, as a unity comprised of religion, art and science. It was only later that this unity split up and became science, religion and art, each existing by and for itself. In our time this separation has reached its culminating point. Things which are essentially united have in the course of cultural development become divided. The nature of man is however such, that for him it is a necessity to experience the three in their "oneness" and not regard them as separate. He can only experience in unity religious science, scientific religion and artistic ideality, otherwise he is inwardly torn asunder. For this reason wherever this division, this differentiation, has reached its highest pitch it has become imperative to find once more the connection between these three spheres. And we shall see how in our teaching we can bring art, religion and science to the child in a unified form. We shall see how the child responds in a living way to this bringing together of religion, art and science, for it is in harmony with his own inner nature. I have therefore had again and again to point out in no uncertain terms that we must strive to educate the child out of a knowledge that he is in truth a being with aesthetic potentialities; and we should neglect no opportunity of demonstrating how in the very first years of life the child experiences religion naturally and instinctively.

All these things, the harmonious coming together of religion, art and science must be grasped in the right way and their value recognised in those teaching methods about which we have still to speak.

LECTURE VIII

Arnheim, 24th July, 1924

You will have seen that in anthroposophical education great value is laid on what lies in the consciousness of the teacher; there must live in his consciousness a knowledge of man that is *whole,* that is complete in itself. Now, as various examples have already shown you, the conception of the world which is usual today is ill-adapted to penetrating deeply into the human being. The following explanation will make my meaning clear. In studying man, we have to distinguish between his constituent parts : firstly his physical body, his physical organisation, then the finer ether or life-body which contains the formative forces, the forces which live in growth and in the processes of nourishment, and which, in the early years of childhood, are transmuted into the forces of memory. Then we have to add everything that the plant does not yet possess, although it, too, has growth and nourishment, and even to some extent lives in memory, in so far as it always retains and repeats its form. The next member of his being man has in common with the animal; it is the sentient body, the astral body, the bearer of sensation. Added to this we have the ego-organisation. These four members we have to distinguish from one another, and in so far as we do this we shall gain a true insight into the being of man and into human evolution.

To begin with man receives his *first* physical body, if I may so express myself, out of the forces of heredity. This is prepared for him by his father and mother. In the course of the first 7 years of life this physical body is cast off, but during this time it serves as a model from which the etheric body can build up the second body. Today people make the things confronting them so frightfully simple. If a ten-year-old child has a nose like his father's they say it is inherited. But it is not so simple as this, for as a matter of fact the nose is only inherited up to the time of the change of teeth. For if the ether body is so strong that it rejects the model of the inherited nose, then in the course of the first seven years its shape will change. If on the other hand the ether body is weak, it will not be able to free itself from the model and at the age of 10 the shape of the nose will still be the same. Looked at from an external point of view it seems as though the concept of heredity might still have the same significance in the second 7 year period as it had in the first 7 years. In such cases people are wont to say: "Truth must be simple." In reality things are very complicated. Concepts formed today are mostly the result of a love of ease rather than the urgent desire for truth. It is therefore of real importance that we learn to look with understanding at this body of formative forces, this etheric body, which gradually in the course of the first 7 years creates the second physical body, that in its turn also lasts for 7 years. The etheric body is therefore a creator of form, a sculptor. And just as a true sculptor requires no model, but works independently, while a bad sculptor makes everything according to the model, so in the first life period, and working towards the second period, the ether body, or body of formative forces, fashions the second physical body of the human being. Our present day intellectuality enables us to acquire knowledge of the physical body; it serves this purpose admirably, and anyone lacking intellect cannot acquire such knowledge. But our university studies can take us no further than this. For the ether body cannot be comprehended by means of the intellect, but rather by pictorial, intuitive perception. It would be immensely important if the teacher could learn to understand the ether body. You cannot say: We surely cannot expect all our teachers to develop clairvoyance and so be able to describe the ether body!—But let the teacher practise the art of sculpture instead of studying the things which are so often studied in University courses. Anyone who really works at sculpture and enters into its formative nature will learn to experience the inner structure of forms, and indeed of just those forms with which the human body of formative forces is also working. Anyone who has a healthy sense of form will experience the plastic, sculptural element only in the animal and human kingdoms, not in the plant kingdom. Just imagine a sculptor who wanted to portray plants by means of sculpture! Out of sheer anger one would feel like knocking him down! The plant consists of the physical body and the ether body; with these it is complete. The animal on the other hand envelops the ether body with the astral body and this is still more the case with man. This is why we can learn to comprehend the human etheric body when, as sculptors, we work our way into the inner structure of the forms of Nature. This, too, is why modelling should take a foremost place in the curriculum of a training college, for it provides the means whereby the teacher may learn to understand the body of formative forces. The following may well be taken as a fundamental principle : A teacher who has never studied modelling really understands nothing about the development of the child. An art of education based on the knowledge of man must inevitably induce a sense of apprehension because it draws attention to such things as these and makes corresponding demands. But it can also induce apprehension because it seems as though one must become frightfully critical, rejecting everything that is common practice.

Just as the ether body works at freeing itself in order to become independent at the time of the change of teeth, so does the astral body work in order to become independent at puberty. The ether body is a sculptor, the astral body a musician. Its structure is of the very essence of music. What proceeds from the astral body of man and is projected into form is purely musical in its nature. Anyone able to grasp this knows that in order to understand the human being a further stage of training must develop receptivity towards an inner musical conception of the world. Those who are unmusical understand nothing whatever about the formation of the astral body in man, for it is fashioned out of music. If therefore we study old epochs of culture which were still built up out of inner musical intuition, if we enter into such oriental epochs of culture in which even language was imbued with music, then we shall find a musical conception of the world entering even into the forms of architecture. Later on, in Greece, it became otherwise, and now, especially in the West, it has become very different, for we have entered an age when emphasis is laid on the mechanical and mathematical. In the Goetheanum at Dornach an attempt was made to go back again in this respect. Musicians have sensed the music underlying the forms of the Goetheanum. But generally speaking there is little understanding for such things today.

It is therefore necessary that we should gain in this way a concrete understanding of the human being and reach the point at which we are able to grasp the fact that man's physiological and anatomical form is a musical creation in so far as it stems from the astral body. Think how intimately a musical element is connected with the processes of breathing and the circulation of the blood. Man is a musical instrument in respect of his breathing and blood circulation. And if you take the relationship between the breathing and the circulation of the blood : 18 breaths in a minute, 72 pulse beats in a minute, you get a ratio of 4 : 1. Of course this varies individually in many ways, but by and large you find that man has an inner musical structure. The ratio 4 : 1 is the expression of something which, in itself an inner rhythmical relationship, nevertheless impinges on and affects the whole organisation in which man lives and experiences his own being, In olden times the scansion of verses was so regulated that the line was regulated by the breath and the metrical foot by the circulation.

Dactyl, Dactyl, Caesura, Dactyl, Dactyl. Four in one, the line expressive of the man.

But what man expresses in language is expressed still

earlier in his form. Whoever understands the human being from a musical aspect knows that sound, actual tones, are working within him. At man's back, just where the shoulder blades meet and from there are carried further into the whole human being, forming and shaping him, are those human forms which are constituted out of the prime or key-note. Then there is a correspondence in the form of the upper arm with the second, and in the lower arm with the third. And because there is a major and minor third—not a major and minor second —we have *one* bone in the upper arm, but *two* in the lower arm, the radius and the ulna; and these correspond to the major and minor third. We are formed according to the notes of the scale, the musical intervals lie hidden within us. And those who only study man in an external way do not know that the human form is constituted out of musical tones. Coming to the hand, we have the fourth and fifth, and then, in the experience of free movement, we go right out of ourselves; then, as it were, we take hold of outer Nature. This is the reason for the particular feeling we have with the sixth and seventh, a feeling enhanced by experiencing the movements of eurythmy. You must bear in mind that the use of the third made its appearance comparatively late in the development of music. The experience of the third is an inward one; with the third man comes into an inner relationship with himself, whereas at the time when man lived in the seventh he experienced most fully the going outwards into the world beyond himself. The experience of giving oneself up to the outer world lives especially strongly in the seventh.

And just as man experiences the inherent nature of music, so the forms of his body are shaped out of music itself. Therefore if the teacher wishes to be a good music teacher he will make a point of taking singing with the children from the very beginning of their school life. This must be done; he must understand as an actual fact that singing induces emancipation; for the astral body has previously sung and has brought forth the forms of the human body. Between the change of teeth and puberty, the astral body frees itself, becomes emancipated. And out of the very essence of music emerges that which forms man and makes him an independent being. No wonder then that the music teacher who understands these things, who knows that man is permeated through and through with music, will quite naturally allow this knowledge to enrich the singing lesson and his teaching of instrumental music. This is why we try not only to introduce singing as early as possible into the education of the child, but also to let those children with sufficient aptitude learn to play a musical instrument, so that they have the possibility of actually learning to grasp and enter into the musical element which lives in their human form, as it emancipates and frees itself.

But all these things will be approached in the right way if only the teacher has the right feeling and attitude towards them. It is important to understand clearly that every training college should in fact be so constituted that its curriculum should run parallel with medical studies at a university. The first approach should lead to the intellectual understanding which can be gained from a study of the corpse; this should lead further to an artistic understanding of form, and it can only be acquired when, side by side with the study of physical anatomy, the student practises modelling. This again should lead to a musical understanding. For a true knowledge of man is not attained unless there is added to the earlier medical studies a comprehension of the part music plays in the world. During his college training the student teacher should acquire an understanding of music, not in a purely external way, but inwardly, so that he is able by means of this inner perception to see music everywhere. Music is truly everywhere in the world; one only has to find it. If however we wish to obtain an understanding of the ego-organisation it is essential to master and make one's own the inner nature and structure of some language.

So you see, we understand the physcial body with the intellect, the etheric body through an understanding of form, the astral body through an understanding of music; while the ego, on the other hand, can only be grasped by means of a deep and penetrating understanding of language. It is just here, however, that we are particularly badly off today, for there is a great deal we do not know. Let us take an example from the German language. In German something is described that rests quietly on our body, is round and has eyes and nose in front. It is called in German *Kopf*, in Italian *testa*. We take a dictionary and find that the translation of *Kopf* is *testa*. But that is purely external and superficial. It is not even true. The following is true. Out of a feeling for the vowels and consonants contained in the word *Kopf*, for instance, I experience the *o* quite definitely as a form which I could draw : it is, as eurythmists know, the rounded form which in front is developed into nose and mouth. We find in this combination of sounds, if we will only let ourselves experience it, everything that is given in the form of the head. So, if we wish to express this form, we make use of larynx and lungs and pronounce the sounds approximating to K-o-pf. But now we can say : In the head there is something which enables one person to speak to another. There is a means of communication. We can impart to another person the content of something which we wish to make known—a will or testament for instance.—If you want to describe the head, not in relation to its round form, but as that which imparts information, which defines clearly what one wishes to communicate, then language out of its own nature gives you the means of doing so. Then you say *testa*. You give a name to that which imparts something when you say *testa*; you give a name to the rounded form when you say *Kopf*. If the Italian wanted to describe roundness, he too would say *Kopf;* and likewise, if the German wanted to express communication, he would say *testa*. But both the Italian and the German have become accustomed to expressing in language something different, for it is not possible to express totally different things in a single word. Therefore we do not say exactly the same thing when we speak the word *testa* or *Kopf*. The languages are different because their words express different things.

Now let us try to enter into the way in which a member of a particular nation lives with the language of his folk-soul. The

German way of living in his language is a way of plastic formation. German language is really the language of sculptural contemplation. That has come about in German because in the whole evolution of speech German is a further continuation of the Greek element up into Central Europe. If you study Italian and the Romance languages in general you find the whole configuration is such that they are developed out of the motor function of the soul. They are not contemplative. Italian has formed itself out of an internal dancing, an internal singing, out of the soul's participation in the whole organism of the body. From this we see how the ego stands within the substance of the Folk-Soul; through making a study of the inner connections, the inner make-up of language, we learn to know how the ego works.

This is why it is necessary for the teacher to acquire not only a feeling for music, but an inner feeling for language—taking as a starting point the fact that in the more modern languages we have only retained soul experiences, experiences of feeling, in the interjections. For instance, when in German we say "etsch!"—it is as though someone had slipped and fallen and we want to express this, together with the amusement it has caused. In the interjections we still have something in language which is felt. In other respects language has become abstract, it hovers above things, no longer lives in them. It must, however, again become living and real. We must learn to wrestle with language, we must feel our ego going right through the sounds. Then we shall feel that it is something different whether we say *Kopf* and thereby have the feeling that we should like to draw the form of the head straight away, or whether we say *testa* and immediately have the feeling that we want to dance. It is just this feeling one's way into the activities of life which must be developed quite specially in the teacher.

If therefore the teacher can accustom himself to regarding the physcial and the soul-spiritual together—for they are indeed one, as I have repeatedly impressed upon you—and if he succeeds in doing this ever more and more, he will not be tempted to enter into abstractions and intellectualities, but he will have the will to keep his teaching and educational practice between the change of teeth and puberty within the sphere of the pictorial. There is nothing more distasteful, when one is accustomed to think pictorially about real things, than to have someone coming and talking intellectually in a roundabout way. This is a frightfully unpleasant experience. For example, one is accustomed to seeing something in life as it actually takes place, one only has the wish to describe it as it is, one is living completely in the picture of it; then somebody comes along with whom one would like to come to an understanding, but he forms his judgment purely on the basis of intellect and immediately begins with : It was beautiful, or ugly, or magnificent or wonderful—all these things are one or the other—and one feels in one's soul as if one's hair were being torn out by the roots. It is especially bad when one would really like to know what the other man has experienced and he simply does not describe it. For instance, I may have made the acquaintance of someone who raises his knee very high when he walks—but this man starts immediately with : "He walks well" or "he has a good carriage." But in saying this he tells us nothing about the other man, only about his own ego. But we do not want to know this; we want an objective description. Today people find this very difficult. Hence they do not describe the things, but the effect the things make upon them, as "beautiful" or "ugly." This gradually enters even into the formation of language. Instead of describing the physiognomy of a face, one says : "He looked awful"—or something of the kind.

These are things which should enter into the deepest part of a teachers' training, to get rid of oneself and to come to grips with reality. If one succeeds in doing this, one will also be able to establish a relationship with the child. The child feels just as I described, that his hair is being pulled out by the roots if the teacher does not get to the point, but speaks about his own feelings; whereas, if he will only keep to what is concrete and real and describe this, the child will enter into it all immediately. It is therefore of great importance for the teacher that he does not overdo—his thinking. I always feel it to be a great difficulty with the teachers of the Waldorf School if they think too much, whereas it gives me real satisfaction when they develop the faculty of observing even the smallest things, and so discovering their special characteristics. If someone were to say to me : "This morning I saw a lady who was wearing a violet dress; it was cut in such and such a fashion and her shoes had high heels" and so on—I should like it better than if someone were to come and say : Man consists of physical body, etheric body, astral body and ego,—for the one proves that he stands firmly in life, that he has developed his etheric body, the other that he knows with his intellect that there is an etheric body etc. But this does not amount to much.

I must express myself drastically in this way so that we learn to recognise what is of the greatest importance in the teacher's training; not that he learns to spin out his thoughts about many things, but that he learns to observe life. That he is then able to make use of such observation in life is something that goes without saying. Everything is ruined, however, if he racks his brains over how he should make use of it. This is why anyone who wishes to describe something arising out of Spiritual Science should make very strong efforts to avoid using ordinary abstract concepts, for by so doing he gets right away from what he really wants to say. And especially it is the case that the impression made on anyone who tries to grasp things in a characteristic way will be such that he learns to describe things in the round, not with sharp edges. Here is a drastic example. To me it is unpleasant to say in certain circumstances : "There stands a pale man." That hurts. On the other hand the sentence begins to breathe and have reality if I say : There stands a man who is pale,—in other words, if I do not give a description in stiff, ordinary concepts, but characterise with ideas that enclose it. And one will find that children have much more inner understanding for things when they are expressed in relative form, than they have for bare nouns qualified by adjectives. Children prefer a gentle way of handling things. When I say to them : "There stands a pale man"—it is just as if I was hitting at something with a hammer; but if I say:

"There stands a man who is pale"—it is like a stroking movement of my hand. Children find it much more possible to adapt themselves to the world if things are presented in this second form rather than by hitting at them. A certain fineness of feeling must be developed in order to make oneself a sculptor in the use of language in order to put it to the service of the art of education. It also lies in the sphere of education as an art if one strives to gain a sufficient mastery of language to enable one to articulate clearly in the classroom and to know when teaching how to emphasise what is important and to pass lightly over the unimportant.

We lay great value on just these kind of things, and again and again in the teachers' conferences attention is drawn to the imponderable in teaching. For if one really studies a class, one notices all sorts of things which can be of immense help. For instance, suppose one has a class of 28 boys and girls and one wants to give these children something which they can make their own, something which will enrich their inner life. It may perhaps be a little poem, or even a great poem. You try to teach this poem to the class. Now you will observe the following : If you let them all recite in chorus, or even a third or half of the class, each child will speak and be able to say it; but if you then test one or other of the pupils in order to see if he can say it alone you will find that he cannot. It is not that you have overlooked him and failed to see that he was silent, for he can speak it perfectly well in chorus with the others. The fact is that a group spirit pervades and activates the class and one can make use of this. So if one really works with the whole class, regarding the children as a chorus, it seems at first that this calls up in them a quicker power of comprehension. One day, however, I had to point out the shadow side of this procedure and so I will now entrust you with a secret. It is this. There are also shadow sides in the Waldorf School ! Gradually one finds one's way and discovers that handling the class as a chorus and allowing the children to speak together goes quite well; but if this is overdone, if one works only with the class, without taking the individual child into account, the result will be that in the end no child by himself will know anything.

We must consider the shadow side of all those things and be clear as to how far we can go, for instance, in handling the class as a chorus and to what extent it is necessary to take the individual child seperately. Here theories do not help. To say that it is good to treat the class as a chorus, or to maintain that things should be done in this or the other way is never any use, because in the complexities of life what can be done in one way can also, given other conditions, be done in another way. The worst that can happen in educational science—which indeed is art rather than science—the worst that can happen is that directions are given which have an abstract character and are based on definitions. Educational instructions should consist solely in this, that the teacher is so guided that he enters with understanding into the development of this or that human being, and by means of the most convincing examples is led to a knowledge of man.

Method follows of itself when we proceed in this way. As an example let us consider method in the teaching of history. To want to teach history to a child before the 9th or 10th year is a quite futile endeavour, for the course of history is a closed book to the child before this age. It is only with the 9th or 10th year—you can observe this for yourselves—that he begins to be interested in individual human beings. If you portray Caesar, or Achilles, Hector, Agamemnon or Alcibiades simply as personalities, allowing what belongs to history to appear only as a background, if you paint the whole picture in this way the child will show the greatest interest in it. It will be evident that he is eager to know more about this sort of thing. He will feel the urge to enter further into the lives of these historical personalities if you describe them in this way. Comprehensive pictures of personalities complete in themselves; or comprehensive pictures of how a meal-time looked in a particular century, and in some other century; describe plastically, pictorially, how people used to eat before forks were invented, how they were accustomed to eat in Ancient Rome; describe plastically, pictorially, how a Greek walked, conscious of each step, aware of the form of his leg, feeling this form; then describe how the people of the Old Testament, the Hebrew people walked, having no feeling for form, but slouching along, letting their arms loose; call up feelings for these quite separate and distinct things which can be expressed in pictures; this will give you the right approach to the teaching of history between the 10th and 12th years.

At this latter age we can take a further step and proceed to historical relationships, for it is only now that the child becomes able to understand such concepts as cause and effect. Only now can history be presented as something that is connected, that has cohesion. Everything that lives in history must, however, be worked out in such a way as to show its gradual development. We come to the concept of growth, of becoming. Call up before you the following picture. We are now living in the year 1924*. Charles the Great lived from 760 until 814, so if the year 800 be taken as the approximate date, we find he lived 1120 years before us. If we imagine ourselves now living in the world as a child and growing up, we can reckon that in the course of a century we can have : son or daughter, father or mother, grandfather and perhaps even a great-grandfather, that is to say 3 or 4 generations following one after the other in the course of a hundred years. We can show these 3 or 4 generations by getting someone to stand up and represent the son or daughter. The father or mother will stand behind, resting their hands on the shoulders of the one in front; the grandfather will place his hands on the shoulders of the father, and the great-grandfather his hands on the shoulders of the grandfather. If you imagine placing son, father and grandfather one behind the other in this way, as people belonging to the present age, and behind them the course of the generations in a further ten centuries, you will get all told 11 times 3 or 4 generations, let us say 44 generations. If therefore you were to place 44 people one behind the other, each with his hands on the shoulders of the one in front the first can be a man of the present day and

* The date of the lectures.

the last can be Charles the Great. In this way you can change the time relationships in history, which are so difficult to realise, into relationships which are purely spatial. You can picture it also in this way : Here you have one man who is speaking to another; the latter turns round and speaks to the one behind, who in turn does the same thing, and so it goes on until you come right back to the time when Peter spoke to Christ. In doing this you get the whole development of the Christian Church in the conversation between the people standing one behind the other. The whole apostolic succession is placed visually before you.

It really amounts to this. One should seize every opportunity of making use of what is pictorial and tangible. This is all the more necessary because in this way one learns to enter into reality, thereby learning also to form everything in accordance with what is real. It is actually quite arbitrary if I place 3 beans before the child, then add another 3 beans and yet another 3 or maybe 4, and then proceed to teach addition : 3 plus 3 plus 4 equals 10. This is somewhat arbitrary. But it is quite another thing if I have a small pile of beans and do not know to begin with how many there are. This accords with the reality of things in the world. Now I divide the pile. This the child understands immediately. I give one part to one child, another part to a second child and a third part to a third child. So you see, I divide the pile, first showing the child how many beans there are altogether. I begin with the sum and proceed to the parts. I can let the child count the beans because that is just a repetitive process, 1, 2, 3 and so on, up to 12. But now I divide them into 4, into 4 more and still another 4. If I begin with the sum and proceed to the addenda the child will take it in quite easily. It is in accordance with reality. The other way is abstract, one just puts things together, one is intellectualistic. It is also more real if I get the child to the point when he must answer the following question : If I have 12 apples and somebody takes them, goes away and only brings 7 back, how many has he lost? Here one starts with the minuend and goes from the remainder to the subtrahend; one does not subtract, but goes from the remainder, that is to say, from what remains as the result of a living process, to what has been taken away.

Thus one's efforts are not everywhere directed towards abstractions, but find their outlet in reality; they are linked with life, they strive after life. This reacts on the child and makes him bright and lively, whereas for the most part the teaching of arithmetic has a very deadening effect. The children remain somewhat dead and apathetic, and the inevitable result of this is the calculating machine. The very fact that we have the calculating machine is a proof of how difficult it is to make the teaching of arithmetic perceptually evident. We must however not only do this, but we must learn to read from life itself.

LECTURE IX

Arnheim, 24th July, 1924

It can be said with truth that what our schools are able to accomplish forms part of the whole culture and development of civilisation. It does so either in a more direct way, in which case it is easy to see how a civilisation comes to expression in its art of education, or it lies unnoticed within it. To be sure, civilisation is always an image of what is done in the schools, only very often this is not observed. We shall be able to characterise this by taking our own epoch as an example, but first we will begin with oriental culture.

We really have very little intimate knowledge about the older oriental culture and what still remains of it. Oriental culture has absolutely no intellectual element; it proceeds directly out of the whole human being, that is the human being in his Oriental form, and it seeks to unite man with man. Only with difficulty does it rise beyond the principle of authority. The forms it takes arise, more out of love, in the way of nature. In the whole nexus of the oriental world we cannot speak of a separated teacher and a separated pupil, as in our case. There you do not have the teacher and educator, but you have the *Dada*. The Dada shows the way : through his personality he represents what the growing human being should absorb. The Dada is the one who shows everything, who teaches absolutely nothing. In oriental culture to teach would have no sense. Herbart, a very famous European educationalist, whose views on educational questions were widely accepted in Central Europe, once expressed himself as follows : I cannot think of an education without teaching. With him everything centred on how one taught. The Oriental would have said : I cannot think of an education based on teaching, because in education, everything which should come to fruition in the pupil is contained in living demonstration and example. This holds good right up to the relationship between the Initiate, the Guru, and the Chela, the Disciple. The latter is not taught, he learns by example.

By entering more deeply into such things, what follows will be more easily understood. All Waldorf School education is directed towards the whole human being. Our purpose is not to separate spiritual and physical education, but when we educate the body—because we do this out of fundamental spiritual principles, which are nevertheless extremely practical—our education reaches even into illnesses with all their ramifications. Our aim is to let the spirit work actively in the body; so that in the Waldorf School physical education is not neglected, but is developed out of the knowledge that the human being is soul and spirit. In every way our education contains all that is required for the training of the body.

Further, one must learn to understand what was understood by the Greeks. Greek education was based on gymnastics. The teacher was a gymnast, that is to say, he knew the significance of human movement. In the earlier Greek epoch it would have been more or less incomprehensible to the Greek if one had spoken to him about the necessity of introducing children to logical thinking. For the Greek knew what was brought about when children were taught health-giving gymnastics—in a somewhat milder way in the case of the Athenians, in a harder, more arduous way in the case of the Spartans. For him it was perfectly clear : "If I know how to use my fingers when taking hold of something, so that I do it in a deft, and not in a clumsy way, the movement goes up into the whole organism and in the agile use of my limbs I learn to think clearly. I also learn to speak well when I carry out gymnastic movements rightly." Everything belonging to the so-called training of spirit and soul in man, everything tending towards abstraction, is developed in a quite unnatural way if it is done by means of direct instruction. Schooling of this kind should grow out of the way in which one learns to move the

body. This is why our civilisation has become so abstract. Today
there are men who cannot sew on a torn-off trouser button.
With us in the Waldorf School boys and girls sit together and
the boys get thoroughly enthusiastic over knitting and crochet;
and in doing this they learn how to manipulate their thoughts.
It is not surprising that a man, however well trained in logical
thinking is nevertheless unable to think clearly, if he does not
know how to knit. In this connection we in our time may
observe how much more mobile the thought world of women
is. One has only to study what has followed the admittance of
women to the university in order to see how much more
mobile the soul-spiritual is in women than in men, who have
become stiff and abstract through an activity which leads away
from reality. This is to be observed in its worst form in the
business world. When one observes how a business man con-
ducts his affairs it is enough to drive one up the wall.

These are things which must once again be understood.
I must know that however much I draw on the board,
children will learn to distinguish the difference between
acute and obtuse angles much better, they will learn to
understand the world much better, if we let them practise
holding a pencil between the big and next toe, making
tolerable and well-formed angles and letters—in other
words, when what is spiritual in man streams out of the
whole body—than by any amount of intellectual, conceptual explanation. In Greek culture care was taken that a
child should learn how to move, how to bear heat and cold, how
to adapt himself to the physical world, because there was a
feeling that the soul-spiritual develops rightly out of a rightly
developed physical body. The Greek, educated as a gymnast,
took hold of and mastered the whole man, and the outer
faculties were allowed to develop out of this mastery. We
today, with our abstract science, are aware of a very important truth, but we know it as an abstraction. When we
have children who learn to write easily with the right hand
we know today that in man this is connected with the centre
of speech situated in the left half of the brain. We observe

the connection between movements of the hand and speaking. If we go further we can in the same way learn through physiology to know the connection between movement and thinking. Today therefore we already know, albeit in a somewhat abstract way, how thinking and speaking arise out of man's faculty of movement; but the Greek knew this in a most comprehensive sense. So the gymnast said : Man will learn to think in a co-ordinated way if he learns to walk and jump well, if he learns to throw the discus skilfully. And when he learns to throw the discus beyond the mark he will also comprehend the underlying logic of the story of "Achilles and the Tortoise"; he will learn to grasp all the remarkable forms of logic, which the Greeks enumerated. In this way he will learn to stand firm in reality. Today we usually think somewhat as follows : Here we have a lawyer, there a client; the lawyer knows things which the client does not know. In Greece, however, because it was quite usual to throw the discus beyond the mark, the Greek understood the following : Assuming that a learned lawyer has a pupil whom he instructs in legal matters, and this pupil is so well taught that he must inevitably win every law-suit, what may ensue? In the event of a law-suit involving both pupil and teacher the position would be this : The pupil would inevitably win and inevitably lose ! As you know, the case is then left hanging in the air ! Thus thinking and speaking developed out of an education based on gymnastics : both were drawn out of the whole human being.

Now let us pass on to the Roman civilisation. There the whole man receded into the background, although something of him still remained in the pose of the Roman. Greek movement was still living, pristine and natural. A Roman in his toga looked very different from a Greek; he also moved differently, for with him movement had become pose. In the place of movement education was directed towards only a part of the human being; it was based on speech, on beautiful speaking. This was still a great deal, for in speech the whole upper part of the body is engaged right down into the diaphragm and the bowels. A very considerable part of man is engaged when he learns to speak beautifully. Every effort was made in education to approach the human being, to make something of the human being. This still remained when culture passed over into mediaeval times. In Greece the most important educator was the gymnast, who worked on the whole man; in the civilisation of Rome the most important educator was the rhetorician. In Greece all culture and world-perspective was based on the beautiful human being, conceived in his entirety. One cannot understand a Greek poem, or a Greek statue if one does not know that the Greek's whole world-perspective was centralised in the concept of man in movement. When one looks at a Greek statue and sees the movement of the mouth, one is led to ask : What is the relationship between this movement and the position of the foot, and so on? It is altogether different when we come to consider Roman Art and culture. There the rhetorician takes the place of the gymnast; there the entire cultural life is centred in oratory. The whole of education is directed towards the training of public speakers, the development of beautifully formed speech, the acquisition of eloquence, and this continues right on into the Middle Ages, when education still worked on man himself. You will see that this is so, if you ask yourselves the following : What was the substance of education in the Middle Ages, to what end and purpose were people educated? There were for instance the Seven Liberal Arts : Grammar, Rhetoric, Dialectic, Arithmetic, Geometry, Astronomy or Astrology, and Music. To take one example : Arithmetic was not practised as it is today, but was taught in order to develop the faculty of working with and entering into the nature of forms and numbers. The study of music enabled the pupil to gain a deeper experience of the whole of life. And astronomy : this helped him to develop the capacity for cosmic thinking. In all these studies the approach was made to man himself. The so-called exact sciences of today played a negligible part in education. That the pupil should understand something of science was held to be of little value. It was considered much more important that he should move and speak well and be able to think and calculate. That he should acquire some sort of ready-made truth was of lesser importance. Hence all culture, the perspective of civilisation developed along lines which produced men able to play a part in public life and affairs and willing to devote themselves to this. Pride was felt in men able to hold their own as public orators, men who were thoroughly representative human beings.

The stream of culture which carried this into later times, in some measure, indeed, right into the present, is the Jesuitical schooling, which, from its first establishment and on into the 18th century, had as its main purpose the training, one might almost say the drilling of human beings, so that they became characters possessing great will-power and as such could be placed into life. From the beginning this was the aim of Jesuitical culture. And it was only in the course of the 19th century, in order not to remain too much behind others, that the Jesuits introduced the exact sciences into their teaching. By these methods the Jesuits developed strong, energetic characters so that today, even if one is an opponent of Jesuitism, one finds oneself obliged to say : If only human beings could be trained to work with such consciousness of purpose for the good, as the Jesuits have trained them to work for the decadence of mankind !

This trend in the development of man first makes its appearance in the Roman civilisation, when out of the gymnast there emerges the rhetorician. We see therefore, in a civilisation which has as its foundation a rhetorical education, what tremendous value is laid on everything in life which can assume world significance in the sphere of rhetoric. Now try to look back on the whole life of the Middle Ages. Everything reveals the fact that life is regarded from the point of view of speech, of rhetorical speech, and this enters into such things as how one should behave, how one man should greet another and so on. All this is not taken for granted, but practised according to a conception of beauty, just as in rhetoric a manner of speaking which conforms to a conception of beauty gives aesthetic

pleasure. Here you see arising everywhere the world-significance of a rhetorical education; while the world-significance
of the Greek education lies in that which comes to expression
in human movement.

And now with the 16th century we come to more modern
times, although in point of fact some preparation for it may
already be seen in the 15th century. Once again something
that still represented much in the human being, in this case the
rhetorical, is pushed into the background. Just as the rhetorical
had pushed back gymnastic training, so now there is a further
step, the rhetorical is pushed back and there is a still greater
limitation, an ever increasing striving after intellectuality. Just
as the Roman educator was the rhetorician, so is our educator
the doctor, the professor. If the gymnast was still a complete
human being, if the rhetorician, when he appeared in public,
wished at least to be a representative human being, so our
professor has ceased to be a human being at all. He denies the
human being and lives more and more in sheer abstractions; all
he is now is a skeleton of civilisation. Therefore, in more
modern times at any rate, the professor adopts the fashion of
dressing like a man of the world; he no longer cares to wear
cap and gown in the lecture room, but dresses in such a way
that it is not apparent immediately that he is merely a skeleton
of civilisation. Ever since the 16th century our entire education
has been focused on the professor. And those who educate in
the sense of this view of what is of importance in the world no
longer take with them into the schools any understanding of
human development and human training, but they impart
knowledge to the child. The child is expected to absorb knowledge; his true development is ignored, but he is expected to
know something; he is expected to acquire learning. Certainly
those in favour of reform in education complain loudly about
this academic attitude, but they cannot get away from it.
Anyone who is fully aware of these things and has a clear
picture in his mind of how a Greek child was educated; anyone
who then turns his attention to what happens in a modern
school where, even though gymnastics are taught, the

development and training of the human being is completely overlooked and scraps of knowledge taken from the sciences are given to the youngest children, must perforce say : It is not only that teachers become skeletons of civilisation, are such already, or if not, regard it as their ideal to become so in one way or another, or at any rate to look upon it as an essential requirement—it is not only that the teachers are like this, but these little children look as if they were small professors. And should one wish to express what constitutes the difference between a Greek child and a modern child, one might well say : A Greek child was a human being, a modern child all too easily becomes a small professor.

This is the great change that has taken place in the world as far as the shaping and development of culture is concerned. We no longer look at the human being himself, but only at what can be presented to him in the way of knowledge, what he should know and bear as knowledge within him. Western civilisation has developed downwards to the point at which the gymnast has descended to the rhetorician and the rhetorician to the professor. The upward direction must be found again. The most important words for modern education at the present time are these : The professor must be superseded. We must turn our attention once more to the whole man. Now consider how this comes to expression in the world-wide significance of education. Not long ago, in Middle Europe, there was a university which had a professor of eloquence. If we go back to the first half of the 19th century we find such professors of eloquence, of rhetorical speech, in many places of learning; it was all that remained of the old rhetoric. Now at the university I have in mind there was a really significant personality who held the post of professor of eloquence. But he would never have had anyone to listen to him if he had been this only, for no one any longer felt the faintest inclination to listen to eloquence. He gave lectures only on Greek archaeology. In the University Register he was entered as "Professor of Eloquence", but actually one could hear only his lectures on Greek archaeology. He had to teach something leading to the acquisition of knowledge, not to the acquiring of a capacity. And indeed this has become the ideal of modern teaching. It leads out into a life in which people know a tremendous amount. Already it hardly seems to be an earthly world any more, where people know so enormously much. They have so much knowledge and so little ability, for that function is lacking which leads from knowledge to ability. For instance, someone is studying for the medical profession, and the time comes for his final examinations. He is now told, quite officially, that as yet he can do nothing, but must now go through years of practical training. But it is absurd that students during their first years are not taught in such a way as to be able to do something from the very beginning. What is the purpose of a child knowing what an addition sum is—if he can only add? What is the purpose of a child knowing what a town is—if he only knows what the town looks like? Wherever we are, the whole point is that we enter into life. And the professor leads away from life, not into it.

The following example can also show us the world-wide significance of education. It was still very apparent in Greece when people came to the Olympic Games. There they could see what it was on which the Greeks laid such value; there they knew that only the gymnast could be a teacher in the schools. It was still similar in the time of the rhetorician. And with us? There are certain people who would like to resuscitate the Olympic Games. This is nothing but a whimsical idea, for in present-day humanity there is no longer any need for them. It is a mere piece of external imitation and nothing is to be gained by it. What penetrates right through the man of today is neither centred in his speech, nor in his studied bearing and gestures, but is something centred in his thoughts. And so it has come about that science now has a positively demonic significance for the world. The cause of this demonic world-wide significance lies in the fact that people believed that things thought out intellectually could further the development of culture. Life was to be shaped and moulded according to theories. This holds good, for instance, in modern Socialism, the whole tenor of which is to fashion life in accordance with such concepts. It was in this way that Marxism came into the world : a few, ready-made unco-ordinated concepts, such as "surplus value" and so on—on these life was to be judged and ordered. Nobody then saw the connections and consequences. But a survey of the totality is absolutely necessary. Let us go to a place in the more westerly part of Middle Europe. Some decades ago a philosopher was teaching there who no longer had anything from life, for he had turned everything into the form of concepts. He believed that life could be formed conceptually. This belief he put forward in his lectures. He had a preference for Russian pupils, of whom he had many, and his philosophy found its practical realisation in Bolshevism. He himself remained an ordinary, upright, middle-class citizen; at that time he had not the faintest inkling of what he was doing in sowing the seed of his philosophy. There grew out of it, nevertheless, the remarkable plant that has blossomed in Bolshevism. The seed of Bolshevism was first sown in the universities of the West; it was sown in the thoughts, in the abstract, intellectualistic education given to the rising generation. Just as someone who knows nothing about plants has no idea what will sprout from a seed, so the people had no idea of what was to grow out of the seed they had planted. They only saw the consequences when the seed began to grow. This is because man no longer understands the great inter-relationship of life.

The world-significance of modern intellectualistic education is that it leads right away from life. We see this if we simply consider quite external things. Before the world war we had books. Well, as you know, one masters the content of these books for just so long as one is reading or making notes on them. Otherwise they remain in the library, which is the coffin of the spiritual life. And only when somebody is perhaps obliged to produce a thesis, does he have to take out the books. This happens in a quite external way, and the person concerned is glad when their content only enters into his head and does not penetrate any further into his being. This is the case everywhere.

But now let us look into life. We have the economic life, the life of rights, and the spiritual life. This all goes on, but we do not think any more about it. We do not think any more at all about inner realities, we think in terms of bank-books. What is still contained in banking of real concern to our economic life—or even to our spiritual life, when, for example, the accounts of schools are prepared? These contain the abstract figures on the balance sheet. And what have these figures brought about in life? They have brought it about that man is no longer personally bound up with what he does. Gradually a point is reached at which it is all one to him whether he is a corn merchant or an outfitter; for trousers mean as much to him as anything else. Now he only calculates what profits are brought in by the business; he only looks at the abstract figures, with an eye for what is likely to prove more lucrative. The bank has taken the place of a living economic life. One draws money from the bank, but apart from this, leaves banking to its economic abstractions. Everything has been changed into abstract externalities, with the result that one is no longer humanly involved in things. When the bank was founded, it was still closely bound up with human beings, because people were still accustomed to standing within the living work of existence, as was the case in earlier times. This was still so in the first half of the 19th century. Then the director of a bank still impressed into it a personal character; he was still actively engaged in it with his will, he still lived with it as a personality. In this connection I should like to relate a little story which describes how the banker Rothschild behaved when a representative of the king of France came to arrange for a State credit. At the time of the ambassador's arrival Rothschild was having a consultation with a dealer in leather. The ambassador, whose visit was concerned with making arrangements for this credit, was duly announced. Rothschild, whose business with the dealer in leather was not yet finished, sent a message, asking him to wait. The minister could not understand how an ambassador from the king of France could possibly be kept waiting and he desired to be announced once more. To this Rothschild said: I am now engaged in business concerning leather, not with state affairs. The minister was now so furious that he burst open the door into Rothschild's room, saying : "I am the ambassador of the king of France!" Rothschild replied : "Please, take a chair." The ambassador, believing that he had not heard rightly, repeated : "I am the ambassador of the king of France."—for he could not conceive that anyone in his position could be offered a chair. Whereupon Rothschild replied : "Take two chairs."

So we see how the personality at that time still made itself felt, for it is there. Is it still there today? It is there in exceptional cases, when, for example, someone breaks through public officialdom. Otherwise, where once there was the personality, there is now the joint-stock company. Man no longer stands as a personality in the centre of things. If one asks : What is a joint-stock company?—the answer may well be : A Society consisting of people who are rich today and poor tomorrow. For things take quite another course today than they did formerly; today they pile up, tomorrow they are again dissolved; human beings are thrown hither and thither in this fluctuating state of affairs, and money does business on its own. So it happens today that a man is glad when he comes into a situation where he can amass a certain amount of money. He then buys a car; later on he buys a second one. Things proceed in this way until his situation changes and now money is scarce. He perforce sells one of the cars and soon after the other one also. This points to the fact that man is no longer himself in control of economic and business life. He has been thrown out of the objective course of business life. I put this forward for the first time in 1908 in Nuremberg, but people did not understand much about it. It was the same in the spring of 1914 in Vienna when I said : Everything is heading towards a great world catastrophe because human beings are now outside the real and concrete and are growing ever more and more into the abstract, and it is clear that the abstract must inevitably lead into chaos. Yet people would not understand it.

Now what must be borne in mind above all else, if one has a heart for education, is that we must free ourselves from the abstract and again work our way into the concrete, realising that everything turns on man himself. Hence emphasis should not be laid too strongly on the necessity for the teacher to have a thorough knowledge of Geography and History, of English or French, but rather that he should understand man, and should build up his teaching and education on the basis of a true knowledge of the human being. Then, if need be, let him sit down and look out in the encyclopaedia the material he requires for his teaching; for if a man does this, but as an educator stands firmly on the ground of a real understanding and knowledge of man, he will nevertheless be a better teacher than one who has an excellent degree, but is totally lacking in true knowledge of the human being.

Then we come to the world-significance of the art of education; then we know that what happens in the school is reflected in the culture of the outer world. This could easily be seen in the case of the Greeks. The gymnast was to be seen everywhere in public life. When the Greek, no matter what he was like in other respects, stood confronting the Agora, it was apparent that he had been educated as a gymnast. In the case of the Romans, what lived in a man's schooling came less into external form.

With us, however, what lives in the school finds its expression only through the fact that life escapes us more and more, that we grow out of life, no longer grow into it; that our account books have their own life to a degree of which we have scarcely an inkling, a life so remote that we no longer have any power over it. It takes its own course; it leads an abstract existence, based only on figures.

And let us look at human beings who are highly educated. At most we recognise them because they wear glasses (or perhaps they don't) on their attenuated little organ. Our present day education has world significance only through the fact that it is gradually undermining the significance of the world.

We must bring the world, the real world into the school once more. The teacher must stand within this world, he must have a living interest in everything existing in the world. Only when the teacher is a man or woman of the world, can the world be brought in a living way into the school. And the world must live in the school. Even if to begin with this happens playfully, then in an aesthetic way, thus finding its expression step by step, it is nevertheless imperative that the world lives in the school. Therefore today it is much more important to draw attention to this approach of mind and heart in our newer education than ever and again to be thinking out new methods. Many of the old methods still in use are good. And what I wanted to say to you is most certainly not intended to put the excellent exponents of education of the 19th century in the shade. I appreciate them fully; indeed I see in the teachers of the 19th-century men of genius and great capacity, but they were the children of the intellectualistic epoch; they used their capacity to work towards the intellectualising of our age. People today have no idea of the extent to which they are intellectualised. Here we touch precisely on the world significance of a new education. It lies in the fact that we free ourselves from this intellectuality. Then the different branches of human life will grow together again. Then people will understand what it once meant when education was looked upon as a means of healing, and this healing was connected with the world significance of the human being. There was a time when the idea, the picture of man was thus: when he was born into earthly existence he actually stood one stage below the human, and he had to be educated, had to be healed in order to rise and become a true man. Education was a healing, was of itself a part of medical practice and hygiene. Today everything is separated. The teacher is placed side by side with the school doctor, externally separated. But this doesn't work. To place the teacher side by side with the school doctor is much as if one looked for tailors who made the left side of a coat, and for others who made the right side, without having any idea who was to sew the two separated parts together. And in the same way, if one takes the measurements of the teacher who is quite unschooled in medicine—the right side of the coat—and then takes the measurements of the doctor, who is quite unschooled in education—the left side of the coat—who is going to sew them together nobody knows! Action must therefore be taken. We must rid ourselves of the "left" tailor and the "right" tailor and replace them once again with the tailor able to make the whole coat. Impossible situations often only become apparent when life has been narrowed down to its uttermost limit, not where life should be springing up and bubbling over.

This is why it is so difficult for us to gain an understanding of what is meant by the Waldorf School. A sectarian striving away from life is the reverse of what is intended. On the contrary, there is the most intensive striving to enter into life.

In such a short course of lectures it is clearly only possible to give a short survey of all that is involved. This I have attempted to do and I hope that it may have proved stimulating. In the final lecture I shall bring the whole course to a conclusion.

LECTURE X*

Arnheim, 24th July, 1924

As I am now coming to the concluding words of this course of lectures on education, I should like first of all to take the opportunity of expressing the deep satisfaction I feel that our friends in Holland, who have set themselves the task of fostering the anthroposophical conception of the world, had the will to arrange this course. Such an enterprise always involves an immense amount of hard work for the organisers. And we ourselves, just because we have very many things to arrange in Dornach, know best of all what goes on behind the scenes on such occasions, all the work that has to be done and how much effort and energy are called for. It is therefore obvious that, before leaving Holland, I should express my very warmest thanks to those who have worked together in order to bring about this whole conference. An educational course has taken place and in my closing words I may perhaps be allowed to say something about the part played by the art of education within the whole sphere of the anthroposophical movement.

An educational art has grown up within the anthroposophical movement, not, so to speak, as something which has found its way into the movement through some abstract intention, but it has arisen with a certain necessity out of the movement itself. Up to now few activities have grown out of the anthroposophical movement so naturally and inevitably as this art of education. In the same way, simply as a matter of course, eurythmy has grown out of the anthroposophical movement through Frau Dr. Steiner, medicine through Frau Dr. Wegman; and educational art, as with the other two, has, I

* Lectures VIII and IX were given on the same day. Lecture X consists of concluding words to Lecture IX.

may venture to say, arisen likewise in accordance with destiny, with karma. For the anthroposophical movement as such is, without any doubt, the expression of something which corresponds to human striving through the very fact that humanity has arisen on the earth.

We need only look back into those ancient times in the evolution of humanity when Mystery Centres were to be found here and there, in which religion, art and science were cultivated out of experiences of the spirit, and we become aware how in those old, sacred centres human beings have had, as it were, intercourse with beings of the supersensible world in order to carry spiritual life into external, physical life. We can pursue our way further into the historical development of humanity and we shall discover ever and again the urge to add what is supersensible to what man perceives with his senses. Such are the perspectives which open up when we penetrate into the historical evolution of humanity and see that what lives in anthroposophy today is ceaseless human striving. As anthroposophy however it lives out of the longings, out of the endeavours of human souls living at the present time. And the following may in truth be said : At the turning point of the 19th to the 20th century it has become possible, if one only has the will, to receive revelations from the spiritual world which will once again deepen the whole world-conception of mankind.

These revelations from the spiritual world, which today must take on a different manifestation from the old Mystery Truths, must accord with modern scientific knowledge. They form the content of anthroposophy. And whoever makes them his own knows also that out of the conditions of our present age many, many more people would come to anthroposophy were it not for the tremendous amount of prejudice, of pre-conceived feelings and ideas, which put obstacles in their path. But these are things which must be overcome. Out of the small circle of anthroposophists must grow an ever larger one. And if we call to mind everything which is living and working in this circle we may perhaps—without in any way wishing to declare that anthroposophy is itself a religious movement—we may perhaps allow a deeply moving picture to rise up before us.

Call to mind the Mystery of Golgotha. Only a hundred years after the Mystery of Golgotha, the most brilliant Roman writer, Tacitus, writes about Christ as if he were someone almost unknown, who had met his death over in Asia. At that time therefore, in the height of Roman civilisation, of Roman spiritual and cultural life, where people were living in the traditions of the previous several thousand years, even there nothing was known of Christ. And it is possible to paint a word-picture of a significant fact : There above is the Roman civilisation—in the arenas, in brilliant performances, in every-thing that takes place in Roman social life, in the life of the state. Below, underground, are those regions known as the catacombs. There many people gather together, gather by the graves of those who, like themselves, were believers in the Mystery of Golgotha. These people must keep everything secret. What goes on under the earth only comes to the surface on those occasions when, in the arena, a Christian is smeared with pitch and burned as an entertainment for those who are civilised citizens. Thus we have two worlds : above, the life of Roman civilisation, based on old, resplendent traditions; below, what is developing in secret under the earth. Let us take the brilliant writer of this epoch. He was able to write what amounts to no more than a brief reference in his notes to the coming into being of Christianity, while his writing table in Rome may well have stood over one of the catacombs without his knowing anything whatsoever about what was taking place beneath him.

Let us take several hundred years later. What earlier had spread over the world in such a spectacular way has now disappeared; the Christian civilisation has risen to the surface of the earth and Christianity is beginning to expand in Europe where previously there had been the Roman culture. Keeping such a picture in view one sees how things actually proceed in the evolution of humanity. And often, when contemplating the present time, one is inclined to say: To be sure,

anthroposophists today do not bury themselves under the
earth; that is no longer customary, or they would have to do it;
externally they find themselves in surroundings as beautiful as
those we have here; but now ask yourselves whether those
from outside, who regard ordinary, normal civilisation as their
own, know more about what is taking place here than the
Romans knew about what was taking place in the catacombs.
One can no longer speak so precisely; the situation has
passed over into a more intellectual sphere, but it remains the
same. And when in thought one looks forward a few hundred
years, one may at any rate indulge in the courageous hope
that the picture will change. Of course, those who know as
little about anthroposophy today as the Romans knew about
Christianity find all this very fantastic; but no one can work
actively in the world who is unable to look courageously at
the path opening out before him. And anthroposophists would
fain look with the same courage at the way which lies ahead.
This is why such pictures rise up in the mind's eye.

From time to time we must certainly turn our attention to
all the opinions about anthroposophy which are held today.
Gradually it has come about that scarcely a week goes by
without the appearance of some sort of antagonistic book
dealing with anthroposophy. The opponents take anthroposophy very seriously. They refute it every week or so, not
indeed so much from different standpoints, for they are not
very inventive, but they nevertheless refute it. It is quite
interesting to observe how anthroposophy is dealt with when
approached in this way. One discovers that very learned people,
or people who should have a sense of responsibility, write books
on some subject or other and introduce what they have read
about anthroposophy. Very often they have not read a single
book whose author is an anthroposophist, but they gather their
information solely from the works of opponents.

Let us take an example. There was once a Gnosis, of which
scarcely anything exists except the Pistis-Sophia, a writing
which does not contain very much and is moreover extremely
difficult to understand. All those who write about the Gnosis

today—for at the present time this realm is very much in the
forefront—know little about it, but nevertheless regard themselves as its exponents. They believe that they are giving some
explanation of the Gnosis when they say it originated out of
Greek culture. I must often think of how it would be if
everything related to anthroposophy went the same way; if, as
many people often wish, all anthroposophical writings were to
be burnt; then anthroposophy would be known as the Gnosis is
known today. It is interesting that today many people say that
anthroposophy is a warmed-up Gnosis. They do not know
anthroposophy because they do not wish to know it, and they
do not know the Gnosis because no external document dealing
with it exists. Nevertheless this is how people talk. It is a
negative example, but it can notwithstanding point in a definite
direction. It can certainly only point to this : Courage and
strength will be needed if anthroposophy is not to go the same
way as the Gnosis, but is to develop so as to unfold its intrinsic
reality. When one looks such things in the face, a feeling of
deep satisfaction arises when one sees all the various undertak-
ings which come about, of which this conference is an example;
for such things taken together should ensure that anthroposophy
will work powerfully into the future. In this educational course
anthroposophy has, as it were, only peeped in through little
windows. Much however has been indicated which may serve to
show how anthroposophy goes hand in hand with reality, how
it penetrates right into practical life. Just because everything
real is permeated with spirit, one can only recognise and
understand reality when one has an eye for the spirit. Of course
it was not possible to speak here about anthroposophy as such.
On the other hand it was perfectly possible to speak about a
sphere of activity in which anthroposophy can work fruitfully :
I mean the sphere of education.

    In the case of eurythmy for instance it was destiny itself that
spoke. Today, looking at things from outside, it might well be
imagined that at a certain moment someone was struck with a
sudden thought : We must have a eurythmy. This was not so,
but at that time there was a family whose father had died.

There were a number of children and the mother was concerned about their welfare. She was anxious that something
worth while should develop out of them. The anthroposophical
movement was still small. The question was put to me : What
might develop out of the children? It was in connection with
this question that the first steps were taken to come to something
in the nature of eurythmy. To begin with the attempt was
confined to the very narrowest limits. So it was out of these
circumstances that the first indications for eurythmy were given.
Destiny had spoken. Its manifestation was made possible
through the fact that there was an anthroposophy and that
someone standing on anthroposophical ground was seeking her
life's career. And soon after—it did not take so very long—the
first pupils who had learned eurythmy themseves became
teachers and were able to carry eurythmy out into the world.
So, with the help of Frau Dr. Steiner, who took it under her
wing, eurythmy has become what it is today. In such a case one
may well feel convinced that eurythmy has not been sought :
eurythmy has sought anthroposophy.

Now let us take medicine. Frau Dr. Wegman has been a
member of the Anthroposophical Society ever since there was a
Society. Her first attempts to heal out of an artistic perception
gave her the predisposition to work medically within the
Anthroposophical Movement. As a whole-hearted anthroposophist she devoted herself to medicine. So here too medicine has
grown out of the being of anthroposophy and today exists
firmly within it because its growth has come about through one
particular personality.

And further. When the waves of the world war had subsided,
people's thoughts turned in all possible directions : Now at last
something really great must happen : now, because human
beings have experienced so much suffering, they must find the
courage to achieve something great; there must be a complete
change of heart. Immense ideals were the order of the day.
Authors of all kinds, who otherwise would have written on
quite other subjects, wrote about "The Future of the State" or
"The Future of the Social Order" and so on. Everywhere

thoughts were turned towards what could now come about out of man himself. On anthroposophical soil many such things sprang up and faded away. Only in the realm of education there was very little to show up to this time. My little book, *The Education of the Child from the Aspect of Spiritual Science,* which appeared more or less at the beginning of the Anthroposophical Movement, was already there and it contained all kinds of indications which could be developed into a whole system of education. It was however not regarded as anything special, nothing more than a booklet that might help mothers to bring up their children. I was constantly asked: Should this child be dressed in blue, or that one in red? Should this child be given a yellow bed-cover or that child a red one? I was also asked what one or another child should eat, and so on. This was an admirable striving in an educational direction but it did not amount to very much.

Then in Stuttgart, out of all these confused ideals, there emerged Emil Molt's idea to found a school for the children of the workers at the Waldorf-Astoria cigarette factory. And Emil Molt, who is present today, had the notion to hand the direction of the school over to me. That was a foregone conclusion. Destiny could not have it otherwise. The school was founded with 150 children drawn from the Waldorf-Astoria factory. It was provided with teachers drawn from the Anthroposophical Movement. The law pertaining to schools in Würtemberg made it possible to choose as teachers men and women who were regarded as suitable. The only condition made was that those who were to become teachers should be able to give some proof in a general way that they were well-fitted for their task. All this happened before the great "freeing of humanity" through the Weimar National Assembly From that time onwards we should no longer have been able to set about things so freely. As it was, we could make a beginning, and it will be possible at least for a few years to maintain the lower classes also.*

---

* It was then possible that a State law might prevent children from entering the school before the fifth class.

Well, then anthroposophy took over the school, or one might equally well say, the school took over anthroposophy. And in a few years the school grew in such a way that children were entered coming from very different backgrounds and belonging to all classes of life. All kinds of people wanted their children to attend Waldorf School, anthroposophists and non-anthroposophists. Very strange opinions were held. Naturally enough parents are fondest of their own children and of course want to send them to an excellent school. To give one example, we have had the following experience. There are many opponents whose opposition is based on scientific grounds; and they know that anthroposophy is so much foolish, unscientific rubbish. Nevertheless they send their children to the Waldorf School. They even discover that the Waldorf School suits their children admirably. Recently two such people visited the Waldorf School and said—But this Waldorf School is really good, we notice this in our children; but what a pity that it is based on "Theosophy". Now the Waldorf School would not be there at all if anthroposophy were not there. So, you see, the judgment of many people amounts to this: It is as if one would say: That is an excellent dancer; the only pity is that he must stand on two legs. Such is the logic of opponents. One cannot do otherwise than say that the Waldorf School is good, for nothing whatever in this school is planned in order to make it a school with a definite "world-conception". In regard to religious instruction, the Catholic children are taught by a Catholic priest, the evangelical children by an evangelical clergyman; and only because in Germany there are a great many non-churchmen who belong to no religious community, are we obliged to arrange for a free religion lesson. Otherwise these children would have had no religious teaching at all. I have great difficulty in finding teachers for these free religion lessons, for they are over-full. There is no inducement whatever to persuade the children to come, for we only want to be a modern school. All we want is to have practical and fundamental principles for the instruction and education. We have no wish to introduce anthroposophy into the school, for we are no sect; what we are concerned with is universally human. We cannot however prevent children from leaving the evangelical and Catholic religion lessons and coming to the free religion lesson. It is not our fault, but they come. And so we have ever and again to see to it that this free religion lesson is continued.

The Waldorf School is growing, step by step. It now has about 800 children and between 40 and 50 teachers. Its growth is well in hand—not so its finances. The financial situation is very precarious. Less than six weeks ago there was no means of knowing whether the financial position would allow the Waldorf School to exist beyond 15th June. Here we have an example which shows clearly how difficult it is today for an undertaking to hold its own in the face of the terrible state of economic affairs in Central Europe, even though it has proved beyond any manner of doubt the spiritual justification for its existence. Again and again, every month, we experience the utmost anxiety as to how we are to make the existence of the Waldorf School economically possible. Destiny allows us to work, but in such a way that the Sword of Damocles—financial need— is always hanging over our heads. As a matter of principle we must continue to work, as if the Waldorf School were established for eternity. This certainly demands a very pronounced devotion on the part of the teaching staff, who work with inner intensity without any chance of knowing whether in three months time they will be unemployed.

Nevertheless anthroposophical education has grown out of the Anthroposophical Society. What has been least sought for is what prospers best. In other words, what the gods have given, not what men have made, is most blessed with good fortune. It is quite comprehensible that the art of education is something which perforce lies especially close to the hearts of anthroposophists. For what is really the most inwardly beautiful thing in the world? Surely it is the growing, developing human being. To see this human being from the spiritual worlds enter into the physical world through

birth to observe how what lives in him, what he has carried down in definite form is gradually becoming more and
more defined in his features and movements, to behold
in the right way divine forces, divine manifestations working
through the human form into the physical world—all this has
something about it which in the deepest sense we may call
religious. No wonder therefore that, wherever there is the striving towards the purest, truest, most intimate humanity, such a
striving as exists as the very foundation of anything anthroposophical, one contemplates the riddle of the growing human being
with sacred, religious fervour and brings towards it all the work
of which one is capable.

That is something which, arising out of the deepest impulses
of the soul, calls forth within the anthroposophical movement
enthusiasm for the art of education. So one may truly say : The
art of education stands within the anthroposophical movement
as a creation which can be nurtured in no other way than with
love. It is so nurtured. It is indeed nurtured with the most
devoted love. And so many venture to say further that the
Waldorf School is taken to the heart of all who know it, and
what thrives there, thrives in a way that must be looked upon
as an inner necessity. In this connection I should like to
mention two facts.

Not so very long ago a conference of the Anthroposophical
Society was held in Stuttgart. During this conference the most
varied wishes were put forward coming from very different
sides. Proposals were made as to what might be done in one or
other sphere of work. And just as today other people in the
world are very clever, so naturally anthroposophists are clever
too; they frequently participate in the cleverness of the world.
Thus it came about that a number of suggestions were inter-
polated into the conference. One in particular was very interesting. It was put forward by pupils who were in the top class
of the Waldorf School and it was a real appeal to the
Anthroposophical Society. The appeal was signed by all the
pupils of the 12th Class and had more or less the following
content : We are now being educated in the Waldorf School in

a genuine, human way; we dread having to enter an ordinary university or college. Could not the Anthroposophical Society also create an anthroposophical university? For we should like to enter a university in which our education could be as natural and human as it is now in the Waldorf School.—The suggestion thrown into the meeting stirred the idealism of the members and as a result the decision was actually taken to found an anthroposophical university. A considerable sum of money was collected, but then, in the time of inflation, millions of marks melted away into pfennigs. Nevertheless there were people who believed that it might be possible to do something of the kind and to do it before the Anthroposophical Society had become strong enough to form and give out judgments. Well, we might certainly be able to train doctors, theologians and so on, but what would they be able to do after their training? They would receive no recognition. In spite of this, what was felt by these childlike hearts provides an interesting testimony to the inner necessity of such education. It was by no means unnatural that such a suggestion was put forward. But, to continue the story, when our pupils entered the top class for the first time we were obliged to take the following measures. We had been able to give the young people only what constituted a living culture, but now they had to find access to the dead culture essential to the Abitur examination.* We had therefore to plan the time-table for the top class in such a way that our pupils could take the Abitur. This cut right across our own curriculum and in our teachers' meetings we found it extraordinarily difficult to reconcile ourselves to putting the examination work as the focal point of the curriculum during the final year of this class. Nevertheless we did this. I had a far from easy time when I visited the class, for on the one hand the pupils were yawning because they had to learn what they must know later for the examination, and on the other hand their teachers often wanted to fit in other things which were not necessary for the examination but which the pupils wanted to know. They had always to be reminded : But you must not say

* The German matriculation.

that at the examination. This was a real difficulty. And then came the examination. The results were passable. However, in the college of teachers and in the teachers' meetings we were— pardon the expression—thoroughly fed up. We said : We have already established the Waldorf School; and now, when we should crown our work during the last school year, we are unable to carry out our intentions and do what the school requires of us. And so, there and then, in spite of everything, we resolved to carry through the curriculum strictly to the end of the final school year, to the end of the 12th class, and moreover to suggest to the parents and pupils that we should add yet another year, so that the examination could be taken then. The pupils accepted this with the greatest willingness for they saw it as a way out which would ensure the realisation of the intentions of the Waldorf School. We experienced no opposition whatever. There was only one request which was that Waldorf School teachers should undertake the coaching for the examination.

You see how difficult it is actually to establish within present day so-called reality something originating purely out of a knowledge of man. Only those who live in a world of fantasy could fail to see that one has perforce to deal with things as they are, and that this gives rise to immense difficulties. And so we have on the one hand the art of education within the anthroposophical movement, something which is loved quite as a matter of course. On the other hand we have to recognise that the anthroposophical movement as it exists in the social order of today is confronted with formidable difficulties when it endeavours to bring about, precisely in the beloved sphere of education, those things of which it perceives the deep inner necessity. We must look reality in the face in a living way. Do not think that it would occur to me for a single moment to ridicule those who out of inner conviction are inclined to say : Well, really, things are not so bad; too much is made of it all, for other schools get on quite all right. No, that is not the point ! I know very well how much work and effort and even spirit are to be found in the schools of today. I fully recognise this. But unfortunately human beings today do not look ahead in their thinking. They do not see the threads connecting education, as it has become in the last few centuries, with what is approaching us with all the violence of a storm, threatening to ravage and lay waste our social life. Anthroposophy knows what are the conditions essential to the development of culture in the future; this alone compels us to work out such methods as you will find in our education. Our concern is to provide humanity with the possibility of progress, to save it from retrogression.

I have described on the one hand how the art of education stands within the anthroposophical movement, but how, on the other hand, through the fact that this art of education is centred in the anthroposophical movement, that movement is itself faced with great difficulties in the public life of today.

When therefore it so happens that to an ever increasing extent a larger circle of people, as has been the case here, come together who are desirous of hearing what anthroposophy has to say on the subject of education, one is thankful to the genius of our time that it is possible to speak about what lies so closely to one's heart. In this particular course of lectures I was only able to give a stimulus, to make certain suggestions. But when one comes down to rock bottom, not all that much has been achieved; for our anthroposophical education rests on actual teaching practice. It only lives when it is carried out; for it intends nothing more nor less than life itself. In actual fact it cannot truly be described, it must be experienced. This is why when one tries to stimulate interest in what must necessarily be led over into life, one has to make use of every possible art of speech in order to show how in the anthroposophical art of education we have the will to work out of the fullness of life. Maybe I have succeeded but ill in this course, but I have tried. And so you see how our education has grown out of anthroposophy in accordance with destiny.

Many people are still living in anthroposophy in such a way that they want to have it only as a world conception for heart and soul, and they look askance at anthroposophy when it widens its sphere of activity to include art, medicine, education and so on. But it cannot be otherwise, for anthroposophy demands life. It must work out of life and it must work into life. And if these lectures on the art of education have succeeded in showing to some small extent that anthroposophy is in no way sectarian or woven out of fantasy, but is something which is intended to stand before the world with the cool reasonableness of mathematics (albeit, as soon as one enters into the spiritual, mathematical coolness engenders enthusiasm, for enthusiasm is a word that is connected with spirit* and one cannot help becoming enthusiastic, even if one is quite cool in the mathematical sense, when one has to speak and act out of the spirit)—even if anthroposophy is still looked upon today as an absurd fantasy, it will gradually be borne in on people that it is based on absolutely real foundations and strives in the widest sense of the words to embody and practise life. And possibly this can be demonstrated best of all today in the sphere of education.

If it has been possible to give some of those who have been present here a few stimulating ideas, then I am content. And our work together will have its best result if all those who have been a little stirred, a little stimulated, find in their common striving a way to continue in the practice of life what these lectures were intended to inspire.

* The German words for enthusiasm and spirit are *Geist* and *Begeisterung*.

List of relevant literature. Published or distributed by Rudolf Steiner Press, except where otherwise stated.

BY RUDOLF STEINER

A Modern Art of Education (13 lectures)
The Spiritual Ground of Education (9 lectures)
The Study of Man (14 lectures)
The Kingdom of Childhood (7 lectures)
The Essentials of Education (5 lectures)
The Education of the Child in the Light of Anthroposophy (single lecture)
Eurythmy as Visible Speech (15 lectures)
A Lecture on Eurythmy

BY OTHER AUTHORS

by A. C. Harwood
The Way of a Child
The Recovery of Man in Childhood (Hodder & Stoughton)
by L. F. Edmunds
Rudolf Steiner Education: the Waldorf Impulse.

All the published works of Rudolf Steiner in English translation and in the original German, also works of other authors on anthroposophy, can be obtained from:
Rudolf Steiner Press & Bookshop, 35 Park Road, London NW1 6XT and Rudolf Steiner Bookshop, 38 Museum Street, London WC1A 1LP

Catalogues are available

COMPLETE EDITION

of the works of Rudolf Steiner in the original German. Published by the *Rudolf Steiner Nachlassverwaltung, Dornach, Switzerland,* by whom all rights are reserved.

General Plan (abbreviated):

A. WRITINGS

I. Works written between the years 1883 and 1925
II. Essays and articles written between 1882 and 1925
III. Letters, drafts, manuscripts, fragments, verses, inscriptions, meditative sayings, etc.

B. LECTURES

I. Public Lectures
II. Lectures to Members of the Anthroposophical Society on general anthroposophical subjects
   Lectures to Members on the history of the Anthroposophical Movement and Anthroposophical Society
III. Lectures and Courses on special branches of work:
   Art: Eurythmy, Speech and Drama, Music, Visual Arts, History of Art
   Education
   Medicine and Therapy
   Science
   Sociology and the Threefold Social Order
   Lectures given to Workmen at the Goetheanum

The total number of lectures amounts to some six thousand, shorthand reports of which are available in the case of the great majority.

C. REPRODUCTIONS and SKETCHES

Paintings in water colour, drawings, coloured diagrams, Eurythmy forms, etc.

––––––––

When the Edition is complete the total number of volumes, each of a considerable size, will amount to several hundreds. A full and detailed Bibliographical Survey, with subjects, dates and places where the lectures were given, is available.

All the volumes can be obtained from the Rudolf Steiner Press in London as well as directly from the *Rudolf Steiner Nachlassverwaltung* (address as above).